DATE DUE

MR 3 1 05			

DEMCO 38-296

An Enquiry Concerning The Intellectual And Moral Faculties, And Literature of Negroes

Paul Finkelman
Series Editor

FREEDOM ROAD
Howard Fast
Introduction by Eric Foner

JOHN RANDOLPH
Henry Adams
Introduction by Robert McColley

THE LIFE OF WASHINGTON
Mason L. Weems
Introduction by Peter S. Onuf

GETTYSBURG
Edited by Earl Schenk Miers and Richard A. Brown
Foreword by James I. Robertson, Jr.

CLOTEL; OR, THE PRESIDENT'S DAUGHTER
William Wells Brown
Introduction by Joan E. Cashin

AN ENQUIRY INTO THE INTELLECTUAL AND MORAL FACULTIES, AND LITERATURE OF NEGROES
Henri Grégoire
Introduction by Graham Russell Hodges

JOHN BROWN
W.E. Burghardt Du Bois
Introduction by John David Smith

An Enquiry Concerning The Intellectual And Moral Faculties, And Literature of Negroes

Henri Grégoire

A new edition with an introduction by Graham Russell Hodges

Translated by
David Bailie Warden

M.E. Sharpe
Armonk, New York
London, England

ok may be reproduced in any fom
e publisher, M. E. Sharpe, Inc.,
1onk, New York 10504.

ging-in-Publication Date

Gregoire, Henri, 1750–1831.
[De la littérature des Nègres, ou, Recherches sur leurs facultés intellectuelles.   English]
An enquiry concerning the intellectual and moral faculties, and literature of Negroes /
Henri Grégoire. — New ed. / with an introduction by Graham Russell Hodges.
p.   cm. — (American history through literature)
Originally published: 1810.
Includes bibliographical references and index.
ISBN 1–56324–912–X (alk. paper). —
ISBN 1–56324–913–8 (pbk. : alk. paper)
1. Blacks.
I. Hodges, Graham Russell, 1946–   .
II. Title.
III. Series.
HT1581.G72   1997
909′.0496—dc20
96–32359
CIP
Printed in the United States of America

The paper used in this publicaton meets the minimum requirements of
American National Standard for Information Sciences—
Permanence of Paper for Printed Library Materials,
ANSI Z 39.48-1984.

BM(c) 10 9 8 7 6 5 4 3 2 1
BM(p) 10 9 8 7 6 5 4 3 2 1

Contents

Series Foreword

Novelists, poets, and essayists often use history to illuminate their understanding of human interaction. At times these works also illuminate our history. They also help us better understand how people in different times and places thought about their own world. Popular novels are themselves artifacts of history.

This series is designed to bring back into print works of literature—in the broadest sense of the term—that illuminate our understanding of U.S. history. Each book is introduced by a major scholar who places the book in a context and also offers some guidance to reading the book as "history." The editor will show us where the author of the book has been in error, as well as where the author is accurate. Each reprinted work also includes a few documents to illustrate the historical setting of the work itself.

Books in this series will primarily fall into three categories. First, we will reprint works of "historical fiction"—books that are essentially works of history in a fictional setting. Rather than simply fiction about the past, each will be first-rate history presented through the voices of fictional characters, or through fictional presentations of real characters in ways that do not distort the historical record. Second, we will reprint works of fiction, poetry, and other forms of literature that are primary sources of the era in which they were written. Finally, we will republish nonfiction such as autobiographies, reminiscences, essays, and journalistic exposés, and even works of history that also fall into the general category of literature.

Paul Finkelman

Introduction

In 1809, the Abbé Henri-Baptiste Grégoire, a leading French abolition-ist, sent a manuscript copy of his latest book, *De la littérature des Nègres,* to Thomas Jefferson, the third president of the United States. Although he criticized Jefferson's thesis about innate black inferiority, published in the southerner's *Notes on the State of Virginia,* Grégoire apparently hoped to gain the American's patronage for a forthcoming English translation of his work. Jefferson, grown testier over the years about his controversial views on slavery and blacks' potential, re-sponded with what he regarded as a "soft answer" to Grégoire. He wrote that his remarks in *Notes on the State of Virginia* were of a personal nature and admitted that he desired a "complete refutation of the doubts I have myself entertained and expressed on the grade of understanding allotted to [African Americans] by nature." In a contem-porary letter to Joel Barlow, however, Jefferson derided Grégoire's study as a collection of fantastic tales and raised suspicions about the quality of the talented blacks cited in the book.[1]

Despite Jefferson's dismissal, Grégoire succeeded in publishing his work in English in the United States in 1810; it was translated by David Bailie Warden, the acting American consul to France. The book, entitled *An Enquiry Concerning the Intellectual and Moral Faculties, and Literature of Negroes; with an Account of the Life and Works of Fifteen Negroes and Mulattoes, Distinguished in Science, Literature and the Arts,* influenced African American intellectuals and abolition-ists, who, long aware of Grégoire's friendliness toward their cause, rapidly internalized his perceptions and methods into their own writ-ings. The book also interested later white sympathizers to the anti-slavery cause. The venerable abolitionist Senator Charles Sumner called Grégoire a "hero of humanity." In this century, Haitians, remembering Grégoire's warmth to the cause of their freedom, commemorated the centennial of his passing. Grégoire's life and works remain significant to studies of slavery and abolition in the age of revolution.[2]

This is the first modern republication of the original translation, which was reprinted in facsimile thirty years ago. Grégoire's book is a seminal contribution to understanding early African American intellectual history. The book deserves wider circulation, which should spur further awareness of French involvement in the trans-Atlantic, multiracial abolitionist movement. Grégoire's life and career epitomize the intellectual and spiritual contours of a movement to end slavery and change the world. In this introduction I reacquaint modern readers with Grégoire's life, comment on the book itself, and suggest ways it influenced African American writers.

~

Henri-Baptiste Grégoire was born 4 December 1750 of petit bourgeois parents in the village of Vého in Lorraine, France. His devout mother sent him first to a Jesuit college. After dissolution of the order, Grégoire completed his education with lay professors who instructed him in enlightenment theories and controversies. Grégoire matured with a restless mind, torn between religious orthodoxy and literary pursuits. He taught for a while; his pupils included Alexandre Dumas *père,* later a famous Afro-French writer and father of another. Ordained at twenty-five, Grégoire secured a modest clerical position. In Lorraine, priestly status insured a small salary, but restrictive regulations prevented significant advancement within church ranks, limiting Grégoire's reasonable ambitions to that of a cure in a small village. Fortunately, he received favor from patrons impressed with his talents and intellectual potential. Grégoire quickly developed social and spiritual interests that gained him national attention.[3]

Grégoire's first essays, published in the late 1770s, advocated toleration of Jews. Although Jews were a tiny minority of the nation's population, intolerance in rural areas such as Lorraine was rooted in depressed agricultural conditions. Discriminatory legislation retarded Jewish civil rights and spurred defensive inclusiveness by Jews. Grégoire's passion for Jewish rights, published in an award-winning book in 1785, was based on his unique theology. Grégoire contended that temporal salvation, by which he meant absorption into the Catholic church, was individual, rather than racial or national. Acceptance of Catholicism was insufficient unless the new adherent led a pious life acceptable to God. Grégoire's duty therefore was to help create the conditions under which Jews would convert to Catholicism and be eligible for salvation determined by God. The contemporary church and civil society were too corrupt in his mind to achieve this, so Grégoire constructed a reform ideology. He urged new regulations to force Jews out of the cities into the more salubrious countryside. There they could discard moneylending, which Grégoire believed irritated French animosities toward Jews. Dispersal into the countryside would dissolve the Jews' defensive need for inclusiveness and encourage their acceptance by the peasantry. Grégoire's anachronistic idealism won him awards but had little immediate effect on national policy toward Jews. His assimilationist views may strike modern observers as insensitive and paternalist, but they were the mark of a man determined to better conditions for oppressed peoples.[4]

Grégoire's ability to push his reform ideology was enhanced in 1789 by his election as a representative from the district of Nancy to the First Estate. There, despite his obscurity, he attained prominence among priests who wished to ally the clergy with the national assembly. His reputation ascendant, Grégoire won a secretaryship in the assembly. Grégoire appealed to insurgent representatives on the eve of the French Revolution to consider Jewish rights. As the assembly hammered out concepts of *nation* and *citizenship,* Jewish questions seemed ancillary. Grégoire was able by 1791 to convince an unwilling assembly to enfranchise French Jews and thus prevent their total exclusion from national citizenship. Although he failed to push through his entire platform, Grégoire maintained private associations with Jews and did help some individuals. He wrote more essays arguing for assimilation and noted the moral, intellectual, and social progress made by acculturated Jews. Similar arguments appeared later in his work on Africans.[5]

Grégoire's unsuccessful bid to overcome French anti-Semitism and gain citizenship for Jews did not end his reform attempts. Fully involved in mercurial French politics, Grégoire enlarged his compass to include rights for blacks and opposition to slavery. His dedication to these causes has earned Grégoire his most lasting fame. Growing out of his interest in Jews as outsiders, Grégoire's work on behalf of mulattoes and blacks quickly outstripped his past causes. His acceptance of black rights was based partly on his modern visions of full citizenship for all, a concept that rested on traditional, Catholic tenets of universal salvation.[6]

Grégoire's initial involvement in the abolitionist movement dated back to 1787, when he joined the Société des Amis des Noirs, which was modeled after the English Slave Trade Committee. Grégoire and his colleagues in the Société des Amis invited Jefferson, then living in Paris, to join them, but he declined. The Société initially concentrated on the slave trade but failed to evoke a significant response in French politics before the Revolution. Unsurprisingly, the monarchy sympathized with French West Indian landowners, made anxious about abolitionist attacks, but were more concerned about the perils of representation in the national assembly. Grégoire became an arbitrator deciding which groups from the slave islands should be represented.

Mulattoes constituted the greatest dilemma in decisions about representation from French West Indian colonies. Of mixed blood, mulattoes were not quite citizens, but they were not slaves either. While a few, primarily children of wealthy planters, were privileged, far more lived restricted lives, and their status was akin to that of free blacks in the United States. At first, the Société des Amis was not particularly interested in mulattoes' fate, desiring more to concentrate on the slave trade. In 1789, however, Grégoire and other members were convinced by the visiting English abolitionist, Thomas Clarkson, of the virtues of abolitionism and full rights for all blacks. Quickly, Grégoire wrote a pamphlet advocating mulatto rights, which he attempted to insert into assembly debates.[7]

The plight of Grégoire's new cause resembled that of his past efforts for Jews. His ideas and writings were passionate but roused little interest among most delegates to the assembly. Fortunately, his political experience in provincial politics prepared Grégoire for trans-Atlantic negotiations. He offered a compromise that would admit the planters to the assembly if they recognized the vote for mulattoes. In a pamphlet propounding the need for mulatto rights, Grégoire characterized slavery as a temporary condition and hoped for a general insurrection that would end it. This viewpoint alarmed the planters, who were aware that blacks listened intently to political debates and used splits in the ruling class (for example, the American Revolution) as opportunities to seize freedom.[8]

His reputation as an abolitionist now established, Grégoire became frustrated by national assembly inaction. On one occasion, he consulted with a young mulatto named Vincent Ogé. Shortly after this meeting, Ogé left for the largest French West Indian colony, Saint-Domingue, where he initiated a rebellion. Implicated by association, Grégoire received some blame. While Grégoire battled planters and indifferent politicians in France, Ogé was only the most visible protagonist in a widening black uprising in Saint-Domingue. Grégoire penned a pamphlet, *Lettre aux citoyens de coleur,* which was circulated throughout Saint-Domingue and, many claimed, fomented the slave rebellion. Worried West Indian planters burned Grégoire in effigy.[9]

In October 1791, Grégoire left Paris for a new post as constitutional bishop of Blois. While he was gone from the capital, political conditions changed rapidly. Groups of radical deputies known as Girondins and The Mountain now vied for power. One result of this renewed radicalism was enfranchisement of free Negroes in the colonies. As tensions mounted in France and planter influence waned, Grégoire, who returned to the assembly in 1792, became even more heavily involved in politics. His efforts and those of other members of the Société des Amis des Noirs were outstripped by events abroad. While the national assembly debated ending the slave trade, civil commissioners sent to Saint-Domingue to restore order suddenly emancipated all slaves. As the French (including Grégoire) gulped, the English and Spanish invaded the island. When Sonthonax and Polverel, the commissioners responsible for emancipation, returned to France, Grégoire chaired a committee to investigate their actions. Over the next two years, as the French and Saint-Dominguen societies were turned upside-down, Grégoire's commission agonized until finally approving Sonthanax's order.[10]

The assembly, now lapsing into the counterrevolution of the Terror, was merely reacting to revolution in Saint-Domingue. As Toussaint L'Ouverture rose to power in Saint-Domingue, French officials saw him as the only hope for stopping the British invasion and conciliating the blacks, who were fearful of re-enslavement. Grégoire strongly urged, with Toussaint's backing, a return of Catholic missionaries to the troubled island. Although Grégoire's plan was held up for several years, it represented the best outreach between French governance and revolutionary blacks. Toussaint wrote Grégoire regularly for advice.

Grégoire, frustrated by politics at home, based his idealism on several centuries of religious negotiation between Christian churches and blacks, who were eager to shake off enslavement. His method, rather than the denial reflected in the postrevolutionary United States, much of it authored by Jefferson, sustained a meeting ground between European and African.[11]

Over the next few years, Grégoire pursued his dreams of a revived colonial church, and at home, he opposed the rise of the Bonapartists. Alone among revolutionary leaders, Grégoire was able to survive French politics, probably because of his clerical status and because his abiding interests in Jews and Africans were issues unthreatening to vying factions in the 1790s. Unlike other members of the Société des Amis, he avoided prison and the guillotine.[12]

In 1802, after Toussaint's arrest, Bonaparte resolved to re-enslave West Indian blacks. After the Treaty of Amiens restored England's colonies to France, Bonaparte declared blacks guilty of treason and sought to wage terror against them. As the assembly approved a restoration of slavery for Martinique and other islands, Bonaparte asked the silent Grégoire, still a member, for his opinion. Grégoire responded that "listening to speeches [favoring restoration of slavery] is sufficient to show they are spoken by whites. If these gentlemen were this moment to change colour they would talk differently."[13] Bonaparte cursed Grégoire publically, while the assembly passed the bill to re-enslave the blacks.

While Grégoire reminded the Bonapartists of their racial culpability, he was active in organizing support for the Haitian revolution and against re-enslavement and in writing about racial issues. In May 1799, he wrote a paper on the intellectual, spiritual, and technical achievements of free blacks, contending that intellectual and moral characteristics depended on environmental more than hereditary or racial background. The tumult in Saint-Domingue prevented any translation of his ideas into practice, but his thoughts formed the basis for his book nearly ten years later.

While Grégoire's society was rocked by revolution, counterrevolution, and colonial slave rebellion, Jefferson's America was consolidating its concept of citizenship and reembracing slavery as its political economy in its southern states. In the 1780s, Thomas Jefferson had observed that the republic would need a revolution now and then to reinvigorate itself. George Washington and the Federalist party, which dominated American politics, quickly disassociated itself from such ideals. Domestically, the Federalists formed a new constitution after Shays's Rebellion of 1787 frightened coastal merchants and financiers. Washington himself led the national army against the Whiskey rebels in 1793. Federalist foreign policy avoided ties with revolutionary France and allied the United States with monarchical Great Britain. By 1800, Jefferson's opposition party was in control; his friend James Monroe was governor of Virginia. The revolutionary fervor of both men had long since passed. The two leaders were aghast when an enslaved blacksmith named Gabriel attempted a mass slave revolt in Richmond in 1800. Monroe ordered Gabriel and his accomplices executed or sold to the West Indies. Although Jefferson believed that the conspiracy indicated the need to emancipate and quickly expel blacks, he did little as Virginia legislators passed legislation to curtail the rights of free blacks.[14]

Such was the atmosphere in which Grégoire approached Jefferson for comment on his new book. Moreover, Grégoire had already alienated Jefferson by his attack in 1809 on an epic poem published in an American magazine, The Columbiad, by Joel Barlow, which the priest had deemed anti-Catholic. In America, Federalists had used Grégoire's letter as anti-Jefferson propaganda. Barlow and Grégoire quickly reconciled, but Jefferson seethed with anger.[15]

The Paris version of De la littérature des Nègres was published in 1808. Desiring an American audience for his work, Grégoire convinced David Bailie Warden, the acting American consul in Paris, to prepare an English translation. Warden was a recently naturalized Scots American who had entered the diplomatic service in 1804 after several years teaching in upstate New York. He served as acting consul until a new officer was appointed. That officer, by coincidence, was Joel Barlow. Warden's shaky political status did not help Grégoire's publication chances in the United States. After Barlow's death in 1814 and before the arrival of William H. Crawford, his successor, Warden again served as acting consul. This time Washington authorities regarded his service as presumptuous, and Warden was dismissed. He remained in France, publishing vast compendiums of information about the United States, and assembled book collections about America, which he sold to such institutions as the New York State Library.[16]

Grégoire was probably unaware of Jefferson's hostility, but it did take him two years to find a small publisher, Thomas Kirk of Brooklyn, who agreed to print the book. I shall return to *An Enquiry* shortly, but first will flesh out the remainder of Grégoire's life. He continued publishing, issuing in 1810 a *Histoire des Sects,* on theological errors of schismatic churches. The work repeated his earlier assertions that true Christians could not tolerate slavery. His praise for English and American antislavery activists irritated the proslavery Napoleon, who ordered all copies of the book seized. Effectively silenced for the duration of Napoleon's rule, Grégoire circulated a supplement for *De la littérature des Nègres* among friends, published a history of domesticity in Germany, and awaited the empire's fall, which did not take place until 1814.[17]

The Bourbon Restoration ushered in a political setting that rendered Grégoire anachronistic. Abolitionists lost favor in France and were identified by their enemies, the planters, as responsible for French defeats. Unable to organize effectively, French abolitionists faltered. The Bourbons did remove the ban on Grégoire's imprints, however. Grégoire again took up the subject of slavery and attacked its French defenders. Quickly the government silenced him as it had before. Grégoire even suffered expulsion from the Royal Institute, of which he had been a founding member. French politics vacillated between a revival of Bonapartism and monarchical restoration, and Grégoire was equally unpopular with both.[18]

Undiscouraged, Grégoire by 1820 determined that overt criticism of French politics was pointless and concentrated on assistance to Haiti. In one of his most remarkable books, *Manuel de piété des hommes de couleur et des Noirs,* Grégoire asserted that God makes exception of no man, a further refutation of Jefferson's pseudoscientific racism, by then increasingly assertive in the United States. Grégoire hoped, however, not to prove human equality, but to convert residents of Haiti (as Saint-Domingue was now called) to Catholicism. Among the most controversial aspects of the book was Grégoire's approval of racial intermarriage. For the rest of his life, Grégoire concentrated on assisting Haitians. He died in 1830.[19]

An Enquiry Concerning the Intellectual and Moral Faculties, and Literature of Negroes remains Grégoire's most famous work, even more than his efforts written during the French Revolution. Aspects of the book are easily identifiable. The book's denial of racial justification of slavery fits well with radical abolitionist thinking of the time. Many of the figures singled out by Grégoire for appreciation in the dedication were well known in European and American intellectual circles. Similarly, most of the African figures were widely recognized. Grégoire's style reflected the political exigencies of the period. He organized the book in a somewhat encyclopedic and pedantic style, which he deliberately employed to confuse censors who watched his literary efforts closely and with suspicion.

In the first section, Grégoire treats prominent themes that build toward his taxonomy of accomplished African Americans. For example, Grégoire questions, in the first two chapters, scientific reasoning about skin color, defends Africans and their home continent, then directly confronts Thomas Jefferson's pseudoscientific racial categorizations. Grégoire, like Jefferson, blames the slave trade for miseries felt by blacks and whites. Unlike the third president, Grégoire claims that religion could assuage the wounds suffered by blacks in the slave trade. Jefferson in turn supported forced repatriation of African Americans back to Africa, regardless of whether they were born there.

Grégoire's method in these chapters harkens back to his early education and his essays on the Jews. Many of the scholars cited are philosophers, travelers, or historians. Evidence is drawn from a variety of periods and sources to refute racist characterizations about innate black inferiority. At the same time, Grégoire plainly sees the road to civilization for Africans, as with Jews and other Europeans, leading straight to the Catholic church: "the Christian religion is the infallible mean of extending and securing civilization." This mixture of Catholic mission and enlightenment scholarship was present in Grégoire's writings of the 1780s and survived through revolution, empire, and restoration.

The impact of recent history on Grégoire's thoughts is contained in the two chapters on "moral qualities of Africans." These chapters represent Grégoire at his most radical. At a time when European philosophers and abolitionists sought sympathy from governments and the public through portraits of "noble Africans," Grégoire emphasized the most revolutionary blacks. After a short section in chapter 3 refuting notions of black idleness, Grégoire casts his attention on Colonels Tacky and Cudjoe, eighteenth-century maroon leaders from the West Indies. Prominently discussed in the chapter are the actions of Ogé and Toussaint L'Ouverture, heroes of the black revolt in Saint-Domingue. Such examples would scarcely arouse sympathy from the Bonaparte government and brought the book very close to banishment. Chapter 4 continues this theme with discussions of the valiant and fierce maroons of Surinam, described in the travel accounts of John Stedman. Clearly what Grégoire regarded as "moral qualities" included the courage to fight fiercely for freedom against oppressors.

The last three chapters of the book consist of Grégoire's discussion of talented African Americans. Before listing African Americans of genius, Grégoire first confronts Jefferson's famous dismissal of black potential in his book *Notes on the State of Virginia.* Jefferson, who fancied himself a philosopher and scientist, made a number of controversial statements about Africans in a section on laws. Writing in Paris in the mid-1780s, the future president reflected: "Comparing them [blacks] by their faculties of memory, reason, and imagination, it appears to me, that in memory they are equal to the whites; in reason much inferior, as I think one could scarcely be found capable of tracing and comprehending the investigations of Euclid; and that in imagination they are dull, tasteless, and anomalous. It would be unfair to follow them to Africa for this investigation. We will consider them here, on the same stage as the whites."[20] In these comments, which dogged Jefferson for the rest of his life, the Virginian also claimed that no "nation among them was ever civilized." Grégoire responds with numerous examples of successful governments from Africa and credits the maroons with self-organization. Grégoire's special insights here come from his radical critique of men like Jefferson, and of his own lifetime sympathetic understanding of blacks' goals. He concludes this chapter with an apt discussion of the Sierra Leone colony, where English philanthropists and republican-minded blacks created a new nation.[21]

The last two chapters of the book, on the literature of blacks, are perhaps the best known. *Literature* here means all of the arts and sciences. In chapter 6, Grégoire mentions black interpreters, guitarists, griots (public speakers), and poets. The names mentioned are lesser known, and one gets the impression that Grégoire was rapidly categorizing people about whom he knew very little but saw fit to mention. That comment is not true for chapter 7, in which Grégoire devotes ample attention to major black literary, political, and military figures of the eighteenth and early nineteenth centuries.

Twelve blacks in all are discussed in chapter 7. They include two military figures (Hannibal and Geoffroy), two linguists (Amo and Derham), a theologian (Capetein), six writers (Othello, Cugoano, Wheatley, Williams, Vassa, and Sancho), and a scientist (Bannaker). With the exception of the little-known Geoffroy, about whom Grégoire doubtless learned in his communications with Haitians, the rest were famous and, save for Hannibal, direct and contemporary refutations of Jeffersonian racism. In at least two instances, in his discussions of Wheatley and Sancho, Grégoire pointedly attacks Jefferson's sour comments on their abilities.

It has been argued that Grégoire lacked confidence that Africa could produce people of genius.[22] It is significant, then, that of the twelve important literary figures in chapter 7, only Bannaker and Williams were unquestionably born in the New World. The rest came from Africa at various stages of their lives and showed their genius after learning a new culture. Their talents, contends Grégoire, were proof that the evils of slavery and the slave trade could not suppress true genius and the desire for freedom. As he notes in his conclusion: "There is nothing useful but what is just: there is no law of nature which makes one individual dependent on another. . . . Every person brings with him into the world his title to freedom."

Grégoire found a ready-made audience for his book among educated free blacks in the northern United States. For free and enslaved African Americans, the book's messages were good news. Although New York State legislators passed a gradual emancipation bill in 1799, slavery was still viable, particularly in Kings County, where the book was published. While slavery slowly died, urban free blacks established a political and religious culture intent on creating a black nationalism and refuting sneers from supremacist whites. Much of this cultural drive came from ministers who used the pulpit to inveigh against slavery and celebrate the recent closing of the international slave trade. Part of nation building was the construction of a history, and Grégoire's gallery of accomplished blacks and his defense of African culture were powerful contributions.[23]

Grégoire's methods and messages dovetailed easily with the writings of this early African American renaissance. Black ministers and activists published commemorative speeches, wrote attacks on slavery, and mused about the significance of Africa. One of the first recognitions of Grégoire comes in Russell Parrott's *An Oration of the Abolition of the Slave Trade, Delivered on the First of January, 1814,* in Philadelphia. Parrott's tone was an example of the influence of Grégoire work. Before, black writings only sought God's will, despairing of human assistance. After 1810, the tone of black literary works is more confident and more aware of the contributions of significant blacks. For example, this method appears in the first history of blacks, which was written by the Presbyterian minister and former slave James W.C. Pennington. In his book, Pennington borrows directly from Grégoire's genealogy of significant black leaders, including discussions of Capetein and Amo, which are quoted almost verbatim from *An Enquiry*.[24]

Grégoire's attack on Jefferson also inspired black writers. David Walker, whose *Appeal* was published in 1829 and argued the necessity of a violent uprising against the southern slave states, used Grégoire's technique of debating Jefferson as the philosopher of American independence and racism.[25] Finally, African American writers used Grégoire in their vexing but necessary arguments against American racists. Alexander Crummell, one of the most sensitive of such critics, recalled, late in the nineteenth century, the pangs of anger he felt over John C. Calhoun's insistence that blacks would never understand classical languages or literature. Crummell, writing during the nadir of race relations in the 1890s, recalled how Grégoire had demonstrated the talent and genius of black Americans, even in the midst of enslavement.[26]

A Note on the Text

This edition of *An Enquiry* is an exact rendition of the 1810 translation, with certain exceptions. Grégoire's note style has been modernized, using numbers rather than symbols. Notes have been placed at the close of each chapter. Original spelling and punctuation has been maintained throughout. This edition was typed by Trudy King and checked by Pamela Conley of Colgate University. All errors are the responsibility of the editor.

Graham Russell Hodges

Notes

1. For discussion of the communications between Grégoire and Jefferson, see Winthrop Jordan, *White Over Black: American Attitudes toward the Negro, 1550–1812* (Chapel Hill, NC, 1968), 453–54, and Ruth F. Necheles, *The Abbé Grégoire 1787–1831: The Odyssey of an Egalitarian* (Westport, CT, 1971). Necheles's book is the sole published biography of Grégoire in English and, though I disagree with some of her conclusions, my dependence on it as a source is clear.

2. Sumner is quoted in Necheles, *The Abbé Grégoire,* 278. For Haitian commemoration see Shelby T. McCloy, *The Negro in France* (Lexington, KY, 1971), 266.

3. Necheles, *The Abbé Grégoire,* 1–4; Emmet Kennedy, *A Cultural History of the French Revolution* (New Haven, CT, 1989), 73–76; Simon Schama, *Citizens: A Chronicle of the French Revolution* (New York, 1989), 169. For Dumas, see McCloy, *The Negro in France,* 167.

4. Necheles, *The Abbé Grégoire,* 11–17; Kennedy, *A Cultural History,* 74.

5. Necheles, *The Abbé Grégoire,* 33–38; Gary Kates, "Jews into Frenchmen: Nationality and Representation in Revolutionary France," in *The French Revolution and the Birth of Modernity,* ed. Ferenc Fehér (Berkeley, CA, 1990), 103–117.

6. See, for example, David Brion Davis, *The Problem of Slavery in the Age of Revolution* (Ithaca, NY, 1975), 111, 140, 143, 147, 188, 344.

7. Necheles, *The Abbé Grégoire,* 58–62; C.L.R. James, *The Black Jacobins: Toussaint L'Ouverture and the San Domingo Revolution* (1938; reprint, New York, 1963), 54. For Jefferson's refusal to join, see Edward Derbeyshire Seeber, *Anti-Slavery Opinion in France During the Second Half of the Eighteenth Century* (1937; reprint, New York, 1971), 160.

8. Necheles, *The Abbé Grégoire,* 63–65; John Chester Miller, *The Wolf by the Ears: Thomas Jefferson and Slavery* (New York, 1977), 10, 17–18, 25–26; Graham Russell Hodges, *The Black Loyalist Directory: African Americans in Exile in the Age of Revolution* (New York, 1995).

9. Necheles, *The Abbé Grégoire,* 97–99. Necheles disputes whether Grégoire's pamphlet affected revolutionary conditions in Saint-Domingue, a characterization with which I do not agree. For Ogé, see Sara Shannon, *"The Horrible Combats": A Document on the Revolution in Saint-Domingue, 1790* (Minneapolis, MN, 1992).

10. Necheles, *The Abbé Grégoire,* 113–120.

11. Necheles, *The Abbé Grégoire,* 147–149. For Toussaint L'Ouverture, see James, *Black Jacobins,* 246. The comments on Jefferson are my own.

12. Shelby T. McCloy, *The Humanitarian Movement, in Eighteenth-Century France* (Lexington, KY, 1957), 261.

13. Quoted in James, *The Black Jacobins,* 340.

14. Miller, *Wolf by the Ears,* 126–28; Douglas Egerton, *Gabriel's Rebellion: The Virginia Slave Conspiracies of 1800 and 1802* (Chapel Hill, NC, 1993).

15. Necheles, *The Abbé Grégoire,* 184–85.

16. "David Bailie Warden," in *Dictionary of American Biography,* 12 vols, ed. Dumas Malone et al. (New York, 1936), 11:443.

17. Necheles, *The Abbé Grégoire,* 186.

18. Necheles, *The Abbé Grégoire,* 204–6.

19. Seeber, *Anti-Slavery Opinion in France,* 177.

20. Thomas Jefferson, *Notes on the State of Virginia,* ed. William Peden (New York, 1954), 139.

21. For Jefferson, see William Stanton, *The Leopard's Spots: Scientific Attitudes toward Race in America, 1815–1859* (Chicago, IL, 1960), 56–58. See Hodges, *The Black Loyalist Directory,* for the latest comment on Sierra Leone.

22. Necheles, *The Abbé Grégoire,* 183.

23. Shane White, *Somewhat More Independent: The End of Slavery in New*

York City, 1770–1810 (Athens, GA, 1991), 51–53. On the creation of a black nationalism, see Sterling Stuckey, *Slave Culture: Nationalist Theory and the Foundations of Black America* (New York, 1987).

24. For Parrott, see *An Oration of the Abolition of the Slave Trade by Russell Parrott at the African Church of St. Thomas* (Philadelphia, 1814) in the compilation of articles and pamphlets in Dorothy Porter, *Early Negro Writing, 1760–1837* (Boston, 1971), 388. For Pennington, see James W.C. Pennington, *Text Book of the Origins and History &ct, &ct of the Colored People* (Hartford, CT, 1841).

25. David Walker, *David Walker's Appeal, in Four Articles: Together with a Preamble, to the Coloured Citizens of the World, but in Particular, and Very Expressly, to those of the United States,* 3d ed. (Boston, 1830).

26. Alexander Crummell, "The Attitude of the American Mind toward the Negro Intellect," in *Destiny and Race, Selected Writings of Alexander Crummell,* ed. Wilson Jeremiah Moses (Amherst, MA, 1992), 291.

Facing page: Slightly reduced facsimile of the original title page.

AN
ENQUIRY
CONCERNING

THE INTELLECTUAL
AND

MORAL FACULTIES, AND LITERATURE
OF

NEGROES;
FOLLOWED WITH AN ACCOUNT OF THE

LIFE AND WORKS
OF

FIFTEEN NEGROES & MULATTOES,
DISTINGUISHED IN

SCIENCE, LITERATURE AND THE ARTS.

———⟨⊛⟩———

BY H. GRÉGOIRE,
FORMERLY BISHOP OF BLOIS, MEMBER OF THE CONSERVATIVE
SENATE, OF THE NATIONAL INSTITUTE, OF THE ROYAL
SOCIETY OF GORTTINGUEN, ETC. ETC.

———⟨⊛⟩———

TRANSLATED

BY D. B. WARDEN,
SECRETARY TO THE AMERICAN LEGATION AT PARIS.

———

BROOKLYN:
PRINTED BY THOMAS KIRK, MAIN-STREET.
———
1810.

Dedication

To all those men who have had the courage to plead the cause of the unhappy blacks and mulattoes, whether by the publication of their works, or by discussions in national assemblies, &c.

Frenchmen

Adanson,[1] *Antony Benezet,* Bernardin St. Pierre, Boissy D'Anglas, *Brissot, Curra, Claviere,* Le Cointe Marsillac, *Condorcet,* Cournand, *Dessessarts, D'Estaing,* Ducis, Dupont de Nemours, La Fayette, *Fauchet, Febrie, Ferrand de Baudieres,* Frossard, Garat, Garran, Genty, Gramagnac, Jacquemin, Bishop of Cayenne, St. John Crevecœur, de Joly, Ladebat, *Lanthenas,* Lescalier, *Mirabeau, Montesquieu, Milscent, Necker, Petion,* Robin, La Rochefoucault, Rochen, Rœderer, *Boucher, St. Lambert,* Sibire, Sieyes, Sonthonax, Tracy, *Turgot,* Viefville Dessessarts.

Englishmen

William Agutter, *Anderson,* David Barclay, Richard Baxter, Mrs. Barbauld, Barrow, *Beattie,* Beaufoy, Mrs. *Behn,* Buttler, Campbell, T. Clarkson, *Cooper,* Charles Crawford, *Thomas Day,* Darwin, Dickson, *Dyer,* Alexander Falconbridge, James Foster, *Fothergill, Charles Fox, George Fox,* Gardenstone, Thomas Gisborne, James Grainger, Grandville Sharpe, Gregory, Rowland Hill, Lord Holland, Hornemann, Horne Took, Hughes, *Francis Hutchinson,* James Jamieson, Lay, Ledyard, Lettsom, Lucas, Luffman, Madison, Mackintosh, Miss Hannah More, Mungo Park, Mason, John Newton, Robert Boucher, Nicholls,

Mrs. Opie, Robert Percival, Pickard, John Philmore, Pinckard, *Pitt*, Pratt, *Price, Priestly, James Ramsey*, Richman, Robert Robinson, Rogers, Roscoe, Ryan, *Seval, Shenstone*, Sheridan, *Smeatham*, William Smith, Southey, Stanfield, Stanhope, *Sterne*, Stone, Rector of Coldmorton, Thelwall, Thompson, Thornton, John Walker, *George Wallis, John Wesley*, Whitchurch, *George Whitfield*, Wilberforce, Miss Helen Maria Williams, *John Woolman*, Miss Yearsley.

Americans

Joel Barlow, James Dana, Dwight, *Franklin*, Humphreys, Imlay, Livingston, Madison, Pearce, William Pinkney, Rush, John Vaughen, D.B. Warden, Elhanan Winchester.

Negroes and Mulattoes

Cugoano, Othello, Phillis Wheatley, Julien Raymond, *Ignatius Sancho*, Gustavus Vasa.

Germans

Blumenbach, Augustus La Fontaine, Oldenborg, Usteri.

Danes

Isert, Olivarius, Th. Thaarup.

Swedes

Afzelius, *Nordenskiold, Wadstrom.*

Hollanders

Peter Paulus, Vos, Wrede.

Italians

The Cardinal *Cibo*, the Abbé Pierre, Tamburini.

Spaniard

Avendano.

Let us not be surprised at not finding here the name of any Spanish or Portuguese writer, except Avendano. None but he, as far as I know, has taken the trouble of proving that the negro belongs to the great family of the human race; and that consequently he ought to fulfil all the duties, and exercise all the rights of this family. On the other side of the Pyrenees, these rights and duties were never problematical; and against whom are we to defend ourselves, if there be no aggressor.[2] It is in our time only, that by a forced interpretation of the bible, a Portuguese has endeavoured to prove the lawfulness of colonial slavery, so unlike to that among the Hebrews, which was a species of domesticity; but this pamphlet of Azerodo, has passed from the shop of the librarian to the river of forgetfulness. Such also in Poland, has been the fate of the pamphlets of the trinitarian Grabowski, who laboured to prove from the Bible, the right of rivetting irons on the peasants of that country; whilst Joseph Paulikowski[3] and the Abbé Michel Korpowitz, in his sermons[4] demonstrated, and claimed an equality of rights. The friends of slavery are necessarily the enemies of humanity.

In the Spanish and Portuguese settlements, we generally see negroes live like brethren of different complexions. Religion, the source of joy, who wipes the tear from the eye of the sorrowful, and whose hand is ever ready to bestow benefits; religion interposes between the slave and the master, to soften the rigor of authority and the yoke of obedience.

Thus among two colonial powers, they have not composed useless discourses in favour of negroes, for the same reason that in Belgium, before the English Hartlib, there was no treatise on agriculture, because the improved practice of cultivation made books unnecessary.

If I be reproached for inserting the names of certain individuals, whom virtue disowns, I shall answer, that not willing to attenuate the faults of individuals, I do not present them here except under a point of view relative to the amelioration of the condition of the blacks. Every person is left at liberty to exercise his opinion in associating those writers with that class of men of letters, unfortunately very numerous, who are less valuable than their books.

The list we offer, is doubtless very incomplete; it ought to contain distinguished names, which, unknown to me or forgotten, either because their works are anonymous, or have escaped my researches: I shall, therefore, receive with gratitude any information which may repair these involuntary omissions, rectify errors, and complete the work.

Of philanthropic writers, a great number are no more; on their tombs I present my homage, and I offer the same tribute to individuals still living, who not having abandoned their principles, pursue, with constancy, their noble enterprise, each in the sphere in which Providence has placed him.

Philanthropists! no individual can, with impunity, be just and benevolent. At the birth of time, war commenced between virtue and vice, and will not cease but with them. Devoured with the desire to do injury, the wicked are always armed against him who dares to reveal their crimes, and prevent them from tormenting the human race. Against their guilty attempts let us oppose a wall of brass, but let us avenge ourselves by benefits. Let us be active. Life, which is so long for the commission of evil actions, is short for the performance of virtue. The earth steals from under our steps, and we go to quit this terrestrial scene. The corruption of our times carries towards posterity all the elements of slavery and crimes. Nevertheless, when we repose in the tomb, some honest men, escaping the contagion, will become the representatives of Providence. Let us leave to them the honourable task of defending liberty and misfortune; from the bosom of eternity we applaud their efforts, and they shall doubtless be blest by the common Father of all, who in men, whatever be their colour, acknowledges his work, and loves them as his children.

Notes

1. The names in italic characters indicate that the writers are dead.
2. *V.* Analyse sur la justice du commerce, du rachat des esclaves de la côte d'afrique, par J.J. d'Acunha de Azérédo Coutinho, 8vo. Londres, 1798.
3. *V.* O Poddanych polskich, c'est-à-dire, des paysans polonais, par Joseph Paulikowski. 8vo. Roku, 1788.
4. *V.* Kazania X. Michala Karpowicza, W. Róz'nych ocolicznosciach Miané, c'est-à-dire, Sermons de l'abbé Karpowicz, 3 vol. in-12, W. Krakovie 1806. V. surtout les second et troisième volumes.

Translator's Preface

I recollect to have heard the celebrated professor Millar, of the university of Glasgow, observe, in his course of civil law, "that the mind revolts at the idea of a serious discussion on the subject of slavery. Every individual, whatever be his country or complexion, is entitled to freedom. The happiness of the poor man is of as much importance as that of the rich. No man has a right to reduce another to the condition of the brute. No individual can sell his liberty. The bargain is unequal, and ought to be broken. Negro slavery is contrary to the sentiments of humanity and the principles of justice."

Notwithstanding this opinion, embraced by the just and the humane of all countries, the slave trade has been a subject of discussion for more than twenty years in the British parliament; and so distinguished for talents and sophistry, have been some of its abettors, that a refutation of their false reasonings became highly useful, and even necessary. Self-interest, or an ardent desire to amass riches, has such a powerful influence over the mind, that the English and French colonists believed, or affected to believe, that the black color of the negro was a sufficient excuse, not only for making him a slave, but for treating him even worse than the brute.

In 1796, one hundred thousand Africans, most of them kidnapped, were dragged from their habitations, and transported as slaves, to cultivate the soils of the British isles. The Englishman calculates the profits of their sale, or of their labour, without reflecting even for a moment, that these unfortunates have lost their freedom, their relatives, their friends and their country. All the comforts whites can bestow, can never recompence the loss of liberty.

This subject is so ably discussed by our author, that his work must powerfully contribute to hasten in all countries, the abolition of this unjust and inhuman traffic. The plan recently adopted by the government of the United States, and the late decision of the British parliament give room to hope, that at no very distant period, absolute slavery will exist no more.

The learned senator has proven by facts, that blacks not only possess talents, but also those nobler virtues which elevate man in the scale of being. The planter, by torture and hard labour, endeavouring to render the negro as tame and submissive as the brute, creates and fosters in him that revengeful disposition, which has been considered as interwoven in his frame, and peculiar to his species. Why is the slave indolent and vindictive? he has no spur to industry; the product of his labour is not his own. He is almost naked, and his aliment is scanty and unwholsome. In the British islands, three herrings per week, and a small portion of yams constitute his allotted food. By industry and good behaviour united, he cannot disarm the master of his arbitrary power. For him there is no compassion except that of his fellow slave. He is treated as a malefactor, and under the habitual influence of malevolent passions, he naturally pants for revenge. He can hardly say that virtue is his interest. He finds that honour procures him no benefit; industry no reward. At last dejected and sad, after seven or eight years of hard labour and suffering, he sinks under the meanness of his condition, and expires with the hope that his spirit will return to his much loved country.

I beg leave to inform the reader that this translation was made from the manuscript of the author; and with such haste, that an apology for its imperfections is necessary. The only merit I dare to claim, if merit it can be called, is that of not having mistaken the sense of the author.

As this production is the result of a long and deep investigation of the subject, and composed by a man of great erudition and rare virtues, well known in the religious, political and learned societies of different countries, it will doubtless be read with a high degree of interest. Another recommendation is, that no similar work exists.

May the day soon arrive when the defenders of justice in every country, shall have a right like the eloquent Curran to exclaim, "I speak in the spirit of our laws, which makes liberty commensurate with, and inseparable from our soil; which proclaims even to the stranger and the sojourner, the moment he sets his foot upon our native earth, that the ground on which he treads is holy, and consecrated by the genius of *universal emancipation*. No matter in what language his doom may have been pronounced; no matter what complexion incompatible with freedom, an Indian or an African sun may have burnt upon him; no matter in what disastrous battle his liberty may have been cloven down; no matter with what solemnities he may have been devoted on the altar of slavery: the first moment he touches our sacred soil, the altar and the god sink together in the dust; his soul walks abroad in her own majesty; his body swells beyond the measure of his chains, that burst from around him, and he stands redeemed, regenerated and disenthralled, by the irresistible genius of *universal emancipation*."[1]

Note

1. Defence of Hamilton Rowan, Esquire.

Chapter I

Concerning the signification of the word Negro. *Ought* all blacks *to be included under this denomination? Difference of opinion concerning their origin. Unity of the primitive type of the human race.*

Under the name of Ethiopian, the Greeks comprehended all men of a black colour. This opinion is founded on passages of Herodotus, Theophrastus, Pausanias, Atheneus, Heliodorus, Eusebius, Flavius Josephus, and the Septuagint,[1] they are so named by Pliny the elder, and by Terence,[2] they were distinguished into two classes, Eastern, and Western or African Ethiopians: or in other words, Indians or Asiatics; but Rome having more immediate relations with Africa, than Greece, insensibly introduced the custom of designating the Blacks by the name of Africans.[3]

Among the moderns, the name of Ethiopia being exclusively applied to a region of Africa, many writers, particularly the Spanish and Portuguese, have employed the word *Ethiopian* to designate the whole race of blacks. Nearly thirty years ago, Erhlen printed, at Strasburg, a treatise *de servis Æthiopibus Europeorum in coloniis Americæ.*[4] The denomination of African prevails, but the use of these two names is equally improper, seeing on the one hand that Ethiopia, the inhabitants of which are not of the deepest black colour,[5] is but a region of Africa, and, on the other, that there are Asiatic blacks. Herodotus names them Ethiopians, with long hair, to distinguish them from those of Africa, whose hair is frizzled;[6] because it was believed formerly that the latter

1

belonged exclusively to Africa, and that the blacks, with long hair, were only found on the continent of Asia. Certain regulations had interdicted their importation into the isles of France and Reunion. But we find, by the narratives of travellers, that on the African continent, as well as at Madagascar, there are also Negroes with long hair. Such are the inhabitants of Bornon in the middle parts of Africa:[7] Such were also the Negro Shepherds of the Isle of Cerné where the Carthagenians had factories.[8] On the other hand, the natives of the Isle of Andaman, in the gulph of Bengal, are blacks with frizzled hair; in different parts of India, the inhabitants of the mountains have almost the same color, form and species of hair. These facts are stated in a learned Memoir of Francis Wilford, associate of the national Institute.[9] He adds, that the most ancient statues of Indian divinities, paint the figure of Negroes. These considerations give support to the opinion that this race formerly bore sway over almost all Asia.

The black color forming the most marked character which separates from the whites, a portion of the human race; less attention has been paid to that difference of conformation which establishes varieties among the blacks themselves. Camper alludes to this, when he says, that Rubens, Sebastien Ricci and Vander-Tempel, in painting the Magi, represented *blacks* and not *negroes*. Thus Camper, and other authors, confine this last denomination to those who have prominent cheeks, thick lips, flat nose and matted hair. But is this distinction between them and those who have long lank hair, founded on reason? The specific character of a people is permanent as long as they live insulated, and it weakens, or disappears by mixture. Can Cæsar's picture of the Gauls, be recognized among the present inhabitants of France? Since the people of our continent have been, if we may so say, blended one into the other, the national characters can hardly be known, either in a physical or in a moral point of view. There is less of the Frenchman, less of the Spaniard or of the German, and more of the European; and, of the Europeans, some have their hair frizzled, others lank, but if, on account of this difference, and some others in stature and conformation, we pretended to mark the extent and limits of their intellectual faculties, would it not excite a smile? We find the same in the variety of the blacks: between individuals, living at the extremities of the line, there exists a remarkable difference which is weakened, or lost in those who inhabit the intermediate regions.

The passages of authors, we have cited, prove that the Greeks had black slaves. This is corroborated by Visconti, who, in the Pio-Clementine Museum, has exhibited a fine figure of the negroes who were employed in the baths.[10] Of these Caylus had already presented me several engravings.

As the Mosaic law shielded men from mutilation, Jahn affirms, in his *Biblical Archæology,* that the Hebrew kings purchased from other nations, many Eunuchs, and particularly blacks,[11] but he has no authority in support of this opinion. It is nevertheless probable that they may have possessed this description of men, when the fleet of Solomon sailed from Ezion-geber to Ophir, whence it carried, says Flavius Josephus, much ivory, apes and *Ethiopians;*[12] or they may have been obtained by means of their communication with the Arabians, if it be true, as Whitaker pretends, in his Review of the Roman History of Gibbon, that, from time immemorial, the Arabians purchased slaves on the coast of Guinea. A fact which cannot be disputed is, that Egypt traded with Ethiopia, and that the Alexandrians were employed in the commerce of negroes.[13] Proofs of this have been furnished by Atheneus and by Pliny the Naturalist, and Ameilhon has referred to these authors in his history of the commerce of the Egyptians.[14] Pinkerton believes that the latter are of Assyrian, or Arabian origin.[15]

Heeren thinks, and apparently with much reason, that they descended from the Ethiopians. The more we ascend towards antiquity, the more resemblance we find between their respective countries: The same writing, the same manners and customs. The worship of animals, still existing among almost all the negro race, was that of the Egyptians; their form was that of the negro, their colour was somewhat whitened by the influence of climate. Herodotus assures us, that the Colchians are a colony of Egyptians, because, like them, they have a black skin and frizzled hair.[16] This testimony invalidates the reasoning of Browne. The expressions of Herodotus, says he, signify only that the Egyptians have a tawny complexion and frizzled hair, when compared with the Greeks, but the text does not mention negroes.[17] To this assertion of Browne, nothing is wanting but the proof. The text of Herodotus is clear and precise.

Every thing concurs to give support to the system of Volney, who recognizes in the Copts, the representatives of the Egyptians; they have the same yellowish and smoky skin, a puffed up visage, a large eye, flat nose, thick lip, in a word the Mulatto figure.[18] The same observations induced Ledyard to believe in the identity of the negroes, and

Copts.[19] The Physician Frank, who accompanied the expedition to
Egypt, supports this opinion by the similarity of usages, such as circumcision and *lexcision* practised among the Copts and negroes;[20]
customs, which according to the report of Ludolphus, are preserved
among the Ethiopians.[21]

Blumenbach has observed in the craniums of mummies, that which
characterizes the negro race. Cuvier does not there find this conformity
of structure. These two imposing testimonies, but apparently contradic-
tory, are conciliated in admitting with Blumenbach, three Egyptian
varieties, of which one represents the figure of the Hindoo; another,
that of the Negro; a third, an Indian of the climate of Egypt; the two
first are confounded by lapse of time;[22] the second, which is that of the
negro, is reproduced, says Blumenbach in the figure of a sphinx. This
is contradicted by Browne; he pretends that the statue of the sphinx is
so degraded, that it is impossible to know its true character;[23] and
Meiners doubts whether the figures of the sphinx, be those of heroes or
evil genii. This opinion is overthrown by an inspection of the sphinxes
delineated by Caylus, Norden, Niehbur and Cassas. They were examined on the spot by the three last, and since by Volney and Olivier.[24]
They discover that the figure is Ethiopian, from which Volney concludes, that to the black race, now slaves, we are indebted for the arts,
sciences, and even for speech.[25]

Gregory, in his *Historical and Moral Essays,* refers us to remote
ages, to shew in like manner, that the negroes are our masters in
science; for the Egyptians, among whom Pythagoras and other Greeks
travelled, to learn philosophy, were in the opinion of many writers, no
other than negroes, whose native features were changed and modified
by the successive mixture of Greeks, Romans and Saracens. If it be
proven that the sciences passed from India to Egypt, is it less true that
to arrive in Europe they crossed the latter country?

Meiners confines himself to the support of the opinion, that we owe
little to the Egyptians, and a man of letters at Caen, has published a
dissertation to develope this position.[26] Already it had for its defender,
Edward Long, the anonymous author of the History of *Jamaica;* who,
in giving to negroes, a character very analagous to that of the ancient
Egyptians, charges the latter with bad qualities, refuses them genius
and taste, disputes their talent for music, painting, eloquence and poetry, and grants them only mediocrity in architecture.[27] He might have
added that this mediocrity is manifest in their pyramids; that those

monuments might be constructed by a simple mason, if the life of an individual were sufficiently long. But without ascribing to Egypt the greatest degree of human knowledge, all antiquity decides in favour of those who consider it as a celebrated school, from which proceeded many of the venerable and learned men of Greece.

Although Long refuses to the Egyptians the praise of genius, he raises them far above negroes, for he reduces the latter to the lowest degree of intelligence.[28] As a bad cause is always supported by arguments of the same nature, he pretends to prove the moral inferiority of negroes, by assuring us that their vermin is black. This observation, he says, has escaped all naturalists.[29] In supposing the reality of this fact, who, but Long, would dare to conclude that the varieties of the human race, have not an identical type, or deny to some an aptitude for civilization.

Those who have wished to disinherit negroes, have called in anatomy to their aid, and the difference of colour gave birth to their first observations. A writer named Hanneman, asserts, that the colour of the negroes proceeded from the curse pronounced by Noah against Ham. Gumilla, in refuting him, loses his time. This question has been discussed by Pechlin, Ruysch, Albinus, Littre, Santorini, Winslow, Mitchil, Camper, Zimmerman, Meckel, the elder, Demanet, Buffon, Somering, Blumenbach, Stanhope Smith,[30] and many others. But how can they agree with regard to the consequences, when they disagree concerning the anatomical facts which ought to serve as their basis?

Meckel the elder, thinks that the colour of negroes is owing to the deep colour of the brain; but Walter, Bonn, Somering, Dr. Gall, and other great anatomists, have found the colour of the brain of negroes to be the same as that of whites.

Barrere and Winslow believe, that the bile of negroes is of a deeper colour than that of Europeans; but Somering discovered it to be of a yellowish green.

Shall we attribute the colour of negroes to that of their reticular membrane? If in some it is black, in others it has a copper or dark colour. This is no more than setting the difficulty at a greater distance. For allowing the hypothesis, that the medullary substance, bile, reticular membrane, are constantly black, the cause remains to be explained. Buffon, Camper, Bonn, Zimmerman, Blumenbach, Chardel, his French Translator,[31] Somering and Imlay, attribute the colour of negroes, and that of other species of the human race, to climate, aided by accessary causes, such as heat and regimen. The learned professor of Goettingen remarks, that in Guinea, not only men, but dogs, birds, and particularly the gallinaceous tribe are black; whilst, near the frozen seas, bears and other animals are all white. Demanet, Imlay, and Stanhope Smith,[32] observe that the descendants of the Portuguese, established at Congo, on the coast of Sierra-Leone, and other parts of Africa are become negroes,[33] and to prove that ocular witnesses, as the first are deceived, it is not enough to deny the fact like the translator of the last work of Pallas.[34]

We know that those parts of the human body the least exposed to the sun, such as the sole of the foot, and between the fingers, are pale; thus Stanhope Smith, after having accumulated facts which prove the influence of climate on the complexion and figure, explains why the Africans on the western coast, under the torrid zone, are more black than those on the eastern; and also, why the same latitude in America, does not produce the same effect. Here the action of the sun is opposed by local causes, which in Africa give it more force. In general the black colour is found between the tropics, and its progressive shades follow the latitude among those, who, very long ago established in a country, have neither been transplanted into other climates, nor crossed by other races.[35] If the savages of North America, and the Patagonians, placed at the other extremity of this continent, have a deeper hue than the people who live near the isthmus of Panama, ought we in explaining this phenomenon to resort to ancient transmigrations, and consult local impressions. S. Williams, author of the history of Vermont, supports this system by observations which prove the connexion between colour and climate. Reasoning from approximative data, he conjectures that to render the black race, by intermarriage, of a white colour, five generations are necessary, each of which being computed at twenty-five years, gives 126 years, and that to make the blacks white without intermarriage, and by the sole action of the climate, 4000 years are necessary, and 600 for the red coloured Indians.[36]

These effects are more sensible among slaves in domestic service, who are accustomed to a milder treatment and a better nourishment; not only their features and physiognomy have undergone a visible change, but their moral habits are also improved.[37]

Besides the uncontested fact that there are Albinos, Somering proves by various observations, that whites have assumed a black and yellow hue, and that negroes have whitened, or become of a pale colour in consequence of disease.[38] In white women with child, the reticular membrane sometimes becomes as black as that of the negresses of Angola. This phenomenon is verified by Cat, and con-firmed by Camper,[39] as an ocular witness; Nevertheless Hunter af-firms, that when the race of an animal whitens, it is a proof of degeneration. But does it follow, that, in the human species, the white variety has degenerated? or is it necessary to say, with Dr. Rush, that the colour of the negroes is the result of a disease become hereditary. He supports his opinion by an experiment made by Beddoes, who almost whitened the hand of an African by immersing it in oxygenated muriatic acid.[40] A journalist proposes to send companies of bleachers to Africa.[41] This pleasantry, which throws no light on the subject, is improper when applied to so distinguished a man as Dr. Rush.

Philosophers are not agreed concerning what part of the human body ought to be considered as the seat of thought and affections. Descartes, Hartley, Buffon, offer each his system. As thought has been generally supposed to reside in the brain, some have concluded that the greatest brains are most richly endowed with talents, and that, as the brain of negroes is smaller than that of the whites, the latter ought to be superior to the former. This opinion is destroyed by recent observa-tions. Most birds, and different quadrupeds and fishes, the mouse, squirrel, marmoret, dolphin, and sea-calf have proportionably the brain more voluminous than that of man.

Cuvier is not willing that the extent of intelligence should be mea-sured by the volume of the brain, but by that of a portion of it, named *hemispheres,* which augments or diminishes, says he, in the same pro-portion as the intellectual faculties of all those beings which compose the animal kingdom. To draw this inference, would it not be necessary to know better the relations of man, his moral state, and how many ages shall perhaps elapse, before we have penetrated this mystery.

"All the difference among nations," says Camper, "consists in a line drawn from the conduits of the ears to the base of the nose, and another right line which touches the eminence of the coronal bone above the nose, and extends to the most prominent part of the jaw bone, it being supposed that the head is viewed in profile. It is not only the angle formed by these two lines, which constitutes the difference of animals, but also that of different nations; and it may be said that nature has in some sort employed this angle to determine the animal varieties, and to advance them, as if by degrees, to the perfection of the finest race of men. This angle is smallest in birds, and it augments in proportion as the animal approaches the human figure.

"I shall notice, for example, (it is Camper who speaks) the heads of the ape race, of which some give an angle of 42 degrees, others, one of 50. The head of the African Negro, as well as that of the Calmuck, makes an angle of 70 degrees, and that of the European, one of 80. This difference of 10 degrees forms the beauty of European heads, because it is an angle of 100 degrees which constitutes the great perfection of antique heads. Such heads, approaching the greatest degree of beauty, resemble most that of the Pythian Apollo, and of the Medusa, by Sosocles, two pieces of statuary unanimously considered as superior to all others in beauty."[42]

This facial line of Camper has been adopted by different anatomists. Bonn says, that he found the angle of 70 degrees in the heads of negresses,[43] and as, on one hand, these differences are nearly constant, and, on the other, as science submits itself to the empire of fashion, this species of observation on the volume, configuration, and protuberance of the cranium, and the expansion of the brain has taken the name of *Cranology,* ever since doctor Gall made it the object of his system, which has been combatted by Osiander, who observes, that it is not new, and says, that it is contained in the Metoscopy of Fuschius, and in the *Fasiculus Medicinæ* of John Ketham. He might also have added, Aristotle, Plutarch, Albert the great, Triumphus, Vieussens, &c.

Gall would also establish, from the structure of the cranium, the pretended moral inferiority of negroes, and when he is opposed by the fact, that the talents of many negroes are incontestible, he answers, that in this case their cranological form approaches the structure of the whites; and reciprocally, that the stupid whites have a conformation similar to that of negroes. I pay ready homage to the talents and amiable qualities of doctor Gall and Osiander,[44] but men the most distinguished may be led astray by hypothesis, or may draw just observations from exaggerated consequences. For example, no one will deny that the president of the academy of arts at London, is a great painter, but how are we to consider West's opinion, that the physiognomy of the Jews approaches that of the goats.[45] It is easy to determine national forms when, in all countries we see remarkable varieties even in passing from village to village? I remarked this particularly in the Voge, as Olivier had done in Persia. Lopez saw at Congo, negroes with red hair.[46]

Admitting that each people has a distinct character, which is reproduced until it is altered, or effaced by eventual mixture, yet who can

fix the lapse of time necessary to destroy the influence of those diversi-
ties hereditarily transmitted, and which are the effect of climate, of
education, of dietetic regimen, or of habit. Nature is so diversified in
her operations, that the most skilful eye is often tempted to class con-
generous plants with different species, nevertheless she admits of but
few primitive types, and in the three kingdoms the fruitful power of the
Eternal has caused to shoot forth an infinite variety which form the
ornament and riches of the globe.

Blumenbach believes, that the Europeans degenerate by a long residence in the two Indies, or in Africa. Somering dare not decide
whether the primitive race of man, which once inhabited some corner
of the earth, be perfected in Europe. Whether it be adulterated in
Nigritia, seeing, that in point of force and activity the conformation of
negroes, with relation to their climate, is as compleat, and perhaps
more so, than that of the Europeans. The negro surpasses the European
in the exquisite keenness of his senses, more particularly in that of
smell. This advantage is common to all those inhabitants of different
countries to whom want has prescribed frequent exercise. Such are the
natives of North America—the *maroons,* negroes of Jamaica, who,
with one glance of the eye, distinguish objects in the woods that are
imperceptible to whites. Their erect form, their bold countenance, and
their manly vigour announce their superiority: they communicate with
each other by sounding the horn, and the variations of sound are such
that they summon each other at a distance, distinguishing each by his
name.[47]

Somering farther observes, that the essential perfection of many
plants is injured by culture. The beauty and short-lived freshness which
they are forced to exhibit in the flowers, often destroy the end for
which nature had designed them. The art of producing double flowers,
which we owe to the Hollanders, almost always deprives the plant of
the faculty of reproduction. Something analagous to this is found
among men, their mind is often improved at the expence of the body,
and reciprocally, for the more the slave is brutalized, the more is he
fitted for manual labour.[48]

It is not denied that negroes have great corporeal strength, and as to
beauty, we may ask whence does it result? Doubtless from the color
and regularity of the features; but on what is this founded? Is white as
a colour, to enter exclusively into what constitutes beauty, whilst this
principle is not applicable to other productions of nature? On this

subject it appears, that each has his prejudices, and we know that different black tribes, presenting the devil in the most unfavorable colour, paint him white.

As to regularity of features, it is one of those complex ideas, whose elements are perhaps still unknown, and concerning which, notwithstanding the efforts of Crouzas, Hutcheson, and father André, principles are yet to be established. In the Manchester memoirs, George Walker pretends to shew what the forms and features universally approved among all people, constitute the essential type of beauty, that which is contested, is then a defect—a deviation of judgment.[49] This is asking from erudition the solution of a physiological problem.

Bosman boasts of the beauty of the negresses of India.[50] Ledyard and Lucas that of the negroes of Jalof.[51] Lobo that of the negroes of Abyssinia.[52] Those of Senegal, says Adanson, are the finest men of Nigritia; their shape is without defect, and there is no maimed amongst them.[53] Cosigny saw, at Goree, negresses of great beauty, of an imposing form with Roman features.[54] Ligon speaks of a negress of the isle of St. Jago, who possessed such a degree of beauty and majesty, that he had never seen her equal.[55] Robert Chasle, author of the voyage of Admiral du Quesne, applies this eulogium to the negresses and mulattoes of all the isles of Cape Vert.[56]

After such testimonies, Jedediah Morse will doubtless find some difficulty in explaining that character of superiority which he sees imprinted on the fact of the white.[57]

Those systems, which suppose an essential difference between negroes and white men, have been adopted, 1st. by those who, by every means seek to materialize man, and to rob him of the dearest hopes of his heart: 2d. By others, who, in the primitive diversity of the human race, seek for an argument against the truth of the narration of Moses. 3d. By men, who interested in colonial culture, seek, in the supposed want of the moral faculties of the negro, another reason for treating him, with impunity, like a beast of burden.

One of those who had been accused of manifesting this opinion, defends himself with warmth. Nevertheless he avows, that in his summary opinions, concerning some regulations made at the colonial assembly, and printed at the Cape, he insists that there are two species of men, the white and the red: that negroes and mulattoes not being of the same species as the white, can no more pretend to natural rights than the ourang outang, and that thus St. Domingo belongs to the white species.[58] It is remarkable that the author, then a corresponding member of the academy of sciences now member of the institute, had precisely at this epoch, as fellow correspondent of the same academy, a mulatto of the isle of France, Geoffroi Lislet, of whom we shall hereafter speak.

The colonial laws did not formally declare, that the slave and the brute are equal, but this was implied. From a multitude of facts I select, 1st, A decision of the council of the Cape, taken from an unsuspected source, the collection of Moreau St. Mery. The declaration of this judgment places negroes and hogs on the same level:[59] 2d, The regulation of police, which, at Batavia prevents slaves from wearing stockings or shoes, and from appearing on the side walks near houses, as they are destined to march with brutes in the middle of the street.[60]

For the honor of learned men who have investigated this subject, we hasten to acknowledge that they have not committed outrage against reason in trying to reduce the blacks below humanity. Even those who would measure the extent of their moral faculties by the size of the brain, disavow the reveries of Kaims and all the inductions which materialism, or cupidity may wish to draw from them.

I have had an opportunity of conversing with Bonn of Amsterdam, who has the finest collection known of human skins; with Blumenbach, who perhaps has the richest of human skulls, with Gall, Meiners, Osiander, Cuvier, and Lacepede, and I seize this occasion of expressing my acknowledgments to those learned men. All, with the exception of one who did not dare to decide, like Buffon, Camper, Stanhope Smith, Zimmerman and Somering admit, in the human race, the unity of the primitive type.

Thus physiology accords with the ideas to which we are constantly led by the study of languages and of history, and with those facts which are revealed in the sacred books of the Jews and Christians. These same authors reject all assimulation of man with the race of apes, and Blumenbach, from repeated observations, denies that the female ape has periodical evacuations, which has been considered as a proof of its similitude with the human species.[61]

Between the head of a wild boar and that of the domestic hog, which are confessedly of the same race, there is more difference than between the head of a negro and that of a white man: but, adds he, between the head of a negro and an ourang-outang, the distance is immense. Negroes being of the same nature as the whites, have the same rights as they to exercise:—the same duties to fulfil. These rights and these duties are antecedent to moral developement. This exercise is doubtless improved, or deteriorated according to the qualities of individuals. But is the enjoyment of social advantages to be graduated by a comparative scale of virtues and talents, on which many of the whites themselves would not find a place?

Notes

1. See Jeremiah 13. 25. Flavius Josephus, Jewish Antiquities 1.8. chapter 7. Theophrastus 22d character, Herodotus, &c.

2. Pliny B. 5. 1. 9. Terence Eunuches, act 1. scene 1.

3. Subito flens Africa nègras procubuit lacerata genas.

4. 4to. Argentorati, 1778.

5. Voyage in Ethiopia; by Poucet, p. 99, &c.

6. Herodotus.

7. Thoughts on the political and commercial relations of the ancient people of Africa, and by Heeren, 8vo. Paris, year 8, vol. II. p. 10. 75.

8. Ibid. vol. I. p. 134. 156. 160.

9. Asiatic Researches, vol. III. p. 355.

10. P. 285. plate 81.

11. Archæologia biblica, &c. a J. Ch. John 8. Vienna, p. 389.

12. Josephus Antiquities, B. viii. ch. 7. p. 2. Hudson in his Latin translation, says Æthiopes in Mancipai. It is not found, but supposed in the text.

13. Atheneus, B. iv. Pliny, 1. 6. 123.

14. P 85.

15. Modern Geography, 4to. London, 1807.

16. Herodotus, B. II.

17. Travels in Africa, by Browne, 4to. and new voyage into Upper and Lower Egypt, by Browne, v. I. ch. 12, and Walkener in the Archives Literaires, p. 10, 84, &c.

18. Voyage in Syria and Egypt, by Volney, new edition, vol. I. p. 10. and the following.

19. Ledyard, vol. I. page 24.

20. Memoir on the commerce of the negroes at Cairo, by Louis Frank, Paris, 1802.

21. Jobi Ludolphus, &c. Historia Æthiopica, fol. 1681.

22. De Generis humani varietate nativa, 8vo. Goettingen, 1794.

23. Brown, ibid.

24. Voyage into the Ottoman Empire, Egypt, Persia, &c. by Olivier, 3 vols. 4to, Paris, 1804–7, vol. II. p. 32. and following.

25. Volney, ibid.

26. Dissertations on the prejudice which attributes to the Egyptians discoveries in science, &c. by Cailly, 8vo. at Caen.

27. History of Jamaica, 3 vols. 4to. London, 1774, vol. II. p. 355, and following, and p. 371, &c.

28. History of Jamaica, 3 vols. 4to. London, 1774.

29. Ibid. vol. II. p. 352.

30. Adversaria Anatomica, decade, 3, p. 26, No. 23. Dissert. de sede et causa coloris Æthiopum et cæterorum hominum, Lugd. Bat. 1737. Mem. de l'acad des Sciences, 1702. Obser. anat. 1724. Ven. Expos. anat. 1743. Amst. vol. III. p. 278. De habitu et colore Æthiopum, Kilon, 1677. Discourse on the origin and colour of negroes, 1764. See his Works translated by Herbel, vol. I. p. 24. 1784. History of French Africa, 2 vols. 8vo. On the physical difference between Negroes and Europeans. De generis humani varietate nativa, edit. 3d, 8vo. Goettingen, 1781.

31. De l'Unitè du Genere humain, by Blumenbach, translated by Chardel.

32. An essay on the cause and variety of complexion and figure in the human species, by the Rev. S. Stanhope Smith 8vo. Philadelphia, 1787. This work is worthy of perusal.

33. A topographical description of the western territory of North America, by G. Imlay, 8vo. London, 1793. 9th letter.

34. Voyage into the southern departments, p. 600. a note.

35. It has been said, in pleasantry, that at Liverpool, where many owners of vessels are enriched by this traffic, they pray God daily not to change the colour of negroes.

36. History of Vermont, by Williams, 1794.

37. *V.* An Essay, &c. p. 20, 23, 34, 58, 77, &c.

38. An Essay, &c. p. 48.

39. Dissertations sur les variétés naturelles qui caractérisent la physionomie, etc. par Camper; traduit par Jansen, in 4to. Paris, 1791, p. 18.

40. Transactions of the American Philosophical Societies.

41. Monthly Review, vol. XXXVIII. p. 20.

42. Opuscules, vol. I, p. 16; and Physical Dissertations on the real difference which the human features present in different countries.

43. Descriptio thesauri ossium Morbosos. Hovii, 1785, p. 133.

44. P. 20 of Chardel.

45. Epigrammata in complures.

46. Relazione del reame di Congo, p. 6.

47. History of the Maroons, from their origin to the establishment of their chief tribe, at Sierra Leone, by B.C. Dallas, 2 vols. 8vo. p. 88, and following.

48. Somering, 74.

49. Vol V. second part.

50. Bosman's Voyage to Guinea, 1705, Utrecht, letter 8.

51. Voyage of Ledyard and Lucas, vol. II. p. 338.

52. Hist. account of Abyssinia, by Lobo, 4to. Paris, 1726, p. 68.

53. Adanson's Voyage in Senegal, p. 22.

54. Cossigny's Voyage to Canton.

55. History of the isle of Barbadoes, by Richard Ligon, in the collection of voyages made in Africa and America, 4to. Paris, 1764, p. 20.

56. Journal of a voyage to the East Indies, squadron of Du Quesne, 3 vol. 12 mo. Rouca, 1721, vol. 1. p. 202.

57. Vol. I. p. 182.

58. By the Baron de Beauvois, p. 6. and 26. Report on the troubles of St.

Domingo, by Garran, 8vo. Paris.

59. Laws and Constitution of the colonies, by Moreau St. Mery, vol. VI, p. 144.

60. Voyage to Cochin China, by Barrow, 2 vols. 8vo. Paris, 1807. vol. II. p. 68, and the following.

61. De generis humani varietate nativa. Nevertheless, according to Desfontaines, the female of the *pitheque* (simia pithecus) has a slight periodical discharge.

Chapter II

Opinions relative to the moral inferiority of Negroes. Discussions on this subject. Of the obstacles which slavery opposes to the developement of their faculties. These obstacles combatted by the christian religion. Of bishops and negro priests.

The opinion of the inferiority of negroes is not new. The pretended superiority of the whites is defended by interested judges of the same colour, whose competency might be questioned, before their decision is attacked. This reminds us of the fable of the lion, who on seeing a picture representing an animal of his species struck to the ground by a man, simply observed, that lions have no painters.

Hume, who in his essay on national character, admits that there are four or five races, affirms that the white man only is improved; that no black has distinguished himself by his actions or by his knowledge,—his translator Estwick,[1] and Chatelux have repeated the same assertion.

Barré-Saint-Venant thinks that if nature has given to negroes some combinations of ideas, which raise them above other animals, she has denied them deep reflection, genius and reason.[2]

We regret to find the same prejudice in a man, whose name is not pronounced amongst us, but with the most profound esteem or merited respect—we mean Jefferson in his "Notes on Virginia."[3] To support his opinion it was not enough to undervalue the talents of two negro writers: it was necessary to establish by argument and by a multitude of facts, that if the situation and circumstances of blacks and whites be the same, the former can never rival the latter.

With regard to the difficulty arising from the circumstance of Epictetus, Terence and Phadro, being slaves (he might have added the names of Locman, Esop, Servius Tullius, &c.) he answers, by a *petitio principii,* saying, that they were whites.

Jefferson attacked by Beattie, has been since opposed by Imlay, his countryman, with considerable warmth, especially concerning Phillis Wheatley. Of her works Imlay transcribes affecting passages, but he also is deceived, in saying to Jefferson, that to cite Terence is aukward, seeing that he was not only an African but a Numidian, and a Negro.[4] It appears that Terence was a Carthaginian. Numidia corresponds to what is now named Mauritania, whose inhabitants, of Arabian descent, having invaded Spain, were the most enlightened people of the middle age.

Besides, Jefferson furnishes arms against himself in his answer to Raynal, who reproaches America for not having produced one celebrated man. When we shall have existed, says this learned American, as a nation, as long as the Greeks before they had a Homer, the Romans a Virgil, or the French a Racine, there will be room for astonishment. We may in like manner say, that when the negroes shall have existed in a state of civilization as long as the inhabitants of the United States, without having introduced such men as Franklin, Washington, Warren, Jefferson, Rittenhouse, Rush, Barlow, Rumford, West, Putnam, Mitchell, Hancock, Alston, Vanderlyn, Copely, Miller, Trumbull, Smith, Barton, Fulton, Edwards, and Ramsay, there will be reason for believing that among them there is a total absence of genius.

Alas! how did Genty write in his work, on the *influence of the discovery of America.* "How can the genius of invention spring up from the bosom of disgrace and misery—where there is no recompence in view—no hope of relief."[5]

In most parts of the regions of Africa, civilization and the arts are yet in their infancy. If it is, that the inhabitants are negroes, explain to us the cause, why whites, or copper coloured men of other countries have remained savage, and even man eaters? Why had not the wandering tribes of hunters of North America, before the arrival of Europeans, attained the rank of Shepherds? Nevertheless their capacity for improvement is not contested; it is readily acknowledged by those who traffic with them. We may consider it as a truth well ascertained that cupidity will always find pretexts to justify their slavery.

The arts originate from natural or from factitious wants—the latter are almost unknown in Africa, and as to the natural wants of nourishment, cloathing and shelter, they are almost nothing on account of the heat of the climate. The first, very restrained, is besides easily satisfied, because nature is there prodigal of her riches: all the recent narratives of travellers have greatly modified the opinion, that the African countries are little more than unfruitful deserts. James Field Stanfield, in his fine Poem, entitled *Guinea,* is no more, in this respect than the echo of Travellers.[6]

The christian religion is the infallible mean of extending and securing civilization. Such has been, and will always be its effects. It was by its influence that our ancestors, the Gauls and Francs ceased to be barbarians, and that the sacred woods were no longer stained with the blood of human sacrifices. It was she who illuminated the African church, formerly one of the most splendid regions of catholicity. When religion forsook these countries they were again plunged in darkness. The historian Long, who thinks that the negroes are incapable of forming great mental conceptions, and who, as we shall see, refutes himself in many passages of his work, and among others concerning Francis Williams, reproaches the negroes for eating wild cats, as if it were a crime, and a circumstance unknown in Europe: he says also, that they are given to superstition,[7] as if Europe was free from this infection, and particularly the country of this historian. We may see in Grose a long and ridiculous enumeration of the superstitious observances of English protestants.[8]

If the superstitious man is to be pitied, he is at least not inaccessable to sound notions. False lights may disappear before the splendour of truth. We may be compared to the earth, whose fertility, as the soil is neglected or cultivated, produces venemous, or salutary plants; whereas a soil completely sterile is an emblem of him who is void of religious principles. The belief in a God, as a rewarder and punisher, can alone secure the probity of a man, who screened from the view of those around him, and having no dread of public vengeance may steal with impunity, or commit every other species of crime. These reflections may lead to the solution of a problem often discussed, namely, which of the two is worse, Superstition or Atheism? Altho' in many individuals, passion stifles every sentiment of justice and probity, yet can we hesitate in our choice between him who to be virtuous thinks it sufficient to act conformably to his belief, and another, who, that he may not be a knave, acts in opposition to his system?

To the slave trade, Barrow attributes the present barbarity of some countries of Africa. The Europeans, to procure slaves there, create and perpetuate a state of constant warfare. Those regions are poisoned by their strong liquors, by every species of debauch, of rapacity, cruelty and seduction. Is there a single vice which is not daily renewed in that country? We have an example under our eyes, in those negroes who are brought to Europe, or transported to our colonies. I am not surprised to read, in Beaver, (who was certainly the friend of negroes, and who, in his *African memoranda* bestows eulogiums on their native virtues and talents) the following words, "I would rather introduce among them a rattle snake than a negro who had lived at London."[9] This exaggerated expression, and which is not very flattering to the whites, shews what individuals may become who are taught every species of depravation, without opposing a single check to overcome its cruel consequences.

Homer tells us, that when Jupiter condemns a man to slavery, he takes from him half his mind. Liberty conducts to every thing that is sublime in genius and virtue, whilst slavery extinguishes all. What sentiments of dignity or of respect, can those mortals have for themselves, who are considered as cattle, and who are often staked, by their masters, at cards or billiards, against some barrels of rice or other merchandize. What can individuals perform when degraded below the condition of brutes, overwrought, covered with rags, famished by hunger, and for the slightest fault torn by the bloody whip of an overseer?

The worthy Curate Sibire, who after having travelled as a successful missionary in Africa and in Europe, has met the fate of many worthy priests, being driven from his ministry by a fanatic Clergy. Sibire says, in ridiculing the colonists, "They have made exaggerated descriptions of the happiness of their negroes, and with colours so captivating that in admiring their picture, we almost regret being free, or desire to be a slave. I would not wish these colonists a similar happiness, although they are too worthy of it.[10] Whom will you persuade, (says he,) that the eternal wisdom can contradict itself, and that the common father of men can become a tyrant like you. If, were it possible, there existed upon earth a man destined as a prey to his equals, it would afford an invincible argument against Providence."[11] We have not seen one of those white impostors change his situation for that of one of his negroes. If slaves be so happy, why before these last years did they transport, annually from Africa, 80,000 blacks to fill the place of those who had sunk under fatigue, misery and despair; for planters acknowledge that a great portion of them die after their arrival in America.[12]

The colonists endeavour, by every means, to pursuade their slaves that they are happy. The slaves support the contrary opinion. Whom must we believe? Why are their looks and recollections constantly turned towards their country? Whence arise these bitter regrets of separation, and this disgust of life? Why that anxiety to attend the funeral of their companions, whom death has freed from bondage? Whence this consoling tradition that their happiness in dying shall be to return to their native land? Whence originate these frequent suicides to hasten their return? If Bryan Edwards has thought fit to deny that this opinion is common among the negroes.[13] He is contradicted by a number of authors, and, among others, by his countryman Hans Sloane, who was well acquainted with the colonies,[14] and by Othello, the negro author.[15]

The inhabitants of *Low-point* and of Carbet; two districts of Martinique, more distinguished for their regard to truth, than other colonists, declared, in 1778, that "Religion only, which gives hopes of a better world, can enable the negroes to support a yoke so contrary to nature; and they thus console this people who see nothing here but labour and chains."[16]

At Batavia, the inhabitants flog their slaves in a mass several times a year; after they are whipt, to prevent gangrene, the wounds are immediately covered with pepper and salt; it is Barrow who announces the fact.[17] His countryman Robert Percival, observes on this occasion, that the slaves of Batavia and of other Dutch colonies to the East, being cruelly treated, and having no defence against the ferocity of their masters, and no hope from the justice of tribunals, seek revenge against their tyrants, against themselves, and the human race, in those homicidal courses named *Mocks,* which are more frequent in those colonies than elsewhere.[18]

Volumes might be filled with the recital of crimes, of which they have been the victims. When the partizans of slavery cannot deny the truth of this, they entrench themselves in saying, that nothing of this kind took place lately, to sully the annals of the colonies. There are doubtless planters who cannot be accused of cruelty, and as we leave to every individual the power of shewing that he belongs to this class, if any should complain as if attacked, like Erasmus, we shall answer, that by this he unveils his conscience.[19] The anecdote is modern of the negro captain, who being in want of water, and seeing his cargo ravaged by mortality, threw the blacks by hundreds into the sea. A fact is recent of another negro captain, who disturbed by the cries of the child of a negress on board, dragged it from its mothers' bosom, and threw it into the waves; the groans of the poor negress annoyed him still more, and if she did not experience a similar fate, it was because this African trader hoped to profit by her sale. I am persuaded, says John Newton, that all mothers worthy of the name, will lament her fate. The same author mentions, that another captain having appeased an insurrection, was long employed in seeking modes of the most refined torture to punish what he called a revolt.[20]

In 1789, we have the following account from Kingston, in Jamaica. "Besides the lash of the whip, with which they tear the flesh of the negroes, they muzzle them to prevent them from sucking those sugar-canes, which are watered with their sweat, and the instrument of iron with which the mouth is compressed, stifles their cries when they suffer under the lash."[21]

In 1795, the Maroons of Jamaica, made the planters tremble. A colonel *Quarrel* proposed to the colonial assembly to go to Cuba, to seek there a pack of devouring dogs. His proposition is received with transport. He departs, arrives at Cuba, and in the recital of this infernal mission, inserts a description of a ball given to him by the marchioness of St. Philippe. He returns to Jamaica with his hunters and his dogs: fortunately neither were of use, as peace had been made with the Maroons. But the intention of those planters ought to be known, who payed largely, and voted thanks to colonel Quarrel, whose name, ever to be execrated, ought to figure with that of Phalaris, Mazentius and Nero. I say this with pain, but truth is more respectable than men. In truth the evidence is against the character of Dallas, for what can we think of him who became the apologist of this measure? There are none, according to his opinion, but arch-sophists, who can censure it. "Did not the Asiatics employ elephants in war? Is not cavalry in use among the nations of Europe? If a man were bitten by a mad dog, would he hesitate to cut off the part attached to save his life." And who are the *biters* and the *mad* but those, who, devoured by a thirst of gold, trampling under feet in both hemispheres, all human and divine laws, have dragged unhappy slaves from Africa, to oppress them in another region. It is then true that the thirst of gold and of power, renders men ferocious, adulterates their reason, and destroys every moral sentiment. If circumstances force them to be just, they boast as benefits, those acts which are prompted by necessity. Colonists! if you had been dragged from your hearths, to undergo the fate of the slave, what would you then say? Bryan Edwards painted negroes as tigers: he accused them of having butchered prisoners, women with child, and infants at the mother's breast.

Dallas in refuting him, refutes himself, and without intention, destroys by facts the false reasonings advanced to justify the use of blood hounds.[22]

Oh! that it had pleased God to cause the waves to swallow up these devourers of human flesh, trained and directed by man against his fellow man. I have heard it asserted, that on the arrival of the dogs at St. Domingo, they delivered to them by way of experiment, the first negro they found. The promptitude with which they devoured this unfortunate—the dogs' reward—rejoiced those white tygers in human form.

Wimphen, who wrote during the revolution, declares, that at St. Domingo the strokes of the whip, and the groans of sufferers, served instead of the crowing of the cock, to mark the hour. He speaks of a woman who threw her cook into an oven, because she had forgotten to make some pastry. Before this fiend, a planter, named Chaperon, had done the same thing.[23]

Innumerable depositions made at the bar of the British parliament, have completely unveiled the crimes of planters. New developements have added, if possible, to this evidence, by the publication of a work, entitled *Horrors of Slavery;*[24] and more recently by the voyages of Pinckard,[25] and of Robin.[26] In reading the last, we find that many creole women have renounced that mildness and modesty which are the patrimonial heritage of their sex. With what singular effrontery do they visit the markets to buy naked negroes, whom they employ in their workshops without giving them clothes. To cover their nakedness they make girdles of moss. Robin reproaches the creole women for exceeding the men in cruelty. Negroes condemned to the lash, are fixed with their face to the earth between four stakes; without emotion they see the blood flow, and look with indifference at the long stripes of skin torn from the body of these unfortunates. Negresses with child are not exempt from this punishment. The only privilege granted to them, is to excavate the earth where their abdomen is to be placed. The white children, daily witnesses of these horrors, serve an apprenticeship to inhumanity, by amusing themselves in tormenting negro children.[27] And notwithstanding, that the cry of humanity has been raised from all quarters against the crimes of the slave-trade and slavery, although Denmark, England and the United States, disown the traffic; among us some are found who solicit its re-establishment, notwithstanding the decrees against it, and these words of the proclamation of the first magistrate to the region of St. Domingo, *"you are all equal and free before God and the republic."*

Those pamphleteers speak without *ceasing of unhappy colonists, and never of unhappy negroes.* The planters repeat, that the soil of the colonies has been watered by *their* sweat, and never utter a word concerning the sweat of their slaves. The colonists, with reason, paint the negroes of St. Domingo, as monsters, who, having recourse to a horrible revenge, butchered the whites; but they never say that the whites provoked this vengeance, by driving negroes into the sea, or causing them to be devoured by dogs. The erudition of the colonists is rich in citations in favour of servitude. None are better acquainted than they, with the tactics of despotism. They have read in Vinnius, that the air renders them slaves; in Fermin, that slavery is not contrary to natural law;[28] in Beckford, that the negroes are slaves by nature.[29]

Hilliard D'Auberteuil, whom the ungrateful colonists caused to perish in a dungeon, because he was suspected of being the friend of mulattoes and free negroes, thus wrote, "interest and safety prompt us to load the blacks with so great contempt, that those who reach the sixth generation, are covered with stains which can never be effaced."[30] Barré St. Venant regrets that they have destroyed the opinion of the superiority of the whites. Felix Carteau, author of a work entitled *Soirees Bermudiennes,* or Evenings in Bermuda, admits as an axiom, this *unalterable supremacy of the white race*—this pre-eminence which is the palladium of our species.[31]

He attributes the ruin of St. Domingo, to the *pride* and *premature pretensions* of *people of colour,* instead of attributing it to the pride and immoderate pretensions of the whites. The author of a voyage in Louisiana, at the close of the last century, is willing to perpetuate the happy prejudice which leads many to hate the negro because he is destined to be a slave.[32] Armed with these blasphemies, they again, without shame, request that new fetters may be forged for Africans. The author of a work, entitled *an examination of slavery in general, and particularly of the slavery of the negroes in the French colonies;* appears to believe that negroes do not receive their life, but upon condition of being slaves, and he pretends that they themselves would vote for slavery.[33]

He regrets the time is no more, when the shadow of the white man made the negroes run. Preacher of ignorance, he is unwilling that the people be instructed, and he honours Montesquieu with his criticism, because he dared to ridicule the infallibility of the colonists. Belu, who wished to restore this abhorred regime, declares that they lacerated the negroes with the strokes of the whip. The bad effects, says he, of this laceration, were prevented by pouring upon the wounds a kind of brine, which increased the pain, but healed them quickly. This fact corresponds with what we have read concerning Batavia. But nothing can equal what is written in his pretended wanderings of negrophilism. An individual named Lozieres, whom, not to believe worse of him, we can only consider as deranged, assures us "that the inventor of the slave-trade merits altars;[34] that by slavery we make men worthy of heaven and of earth."[35] He informs us, that the Guinea masters, when they have slaves attacked with cutaneous disorders, which might injure their sale, give them drugs to strike in the humors, of which the more tardy developement, afterwards occasions horrible ravages.[36]

Slaves are almost entirely delivered to the discretion of their masters. The laws have done everything for the latter, and every thing against the former, who, doomed to legal incapacity, cannot even be admitted to give evidence against the whites. If a black man endeavours to escape, the black code of Jamaica gives the tribunal power to condemn him to death.[37]

Some years since, regulations, less ferocious, substituted in the code of this island, prove how horrible were those that have been annulled; and nevertheless, the new, which are still an outrage against justice, are they put in execution? Dallas, who cites them, acknowledges that in practice much amelioration remains to be made.[38] This avowal leaves us to doubt whether the recent determinations be any thing else than a legislative mocking, intended to silence the expostulations of philanthropists; for the whites always make a common cause against all those who are not of their colour.

Besides cupidity will find a thousand means of eluding the laws. This is the case in the United States, where, notwithstanding the traffic merchant Guineamen is interdicted, cargoes of blacks are brought from the coast of Africa to be sold in the Spanish colonies. They would even touch at a port of the Union, and sell them there, if they did not dread the vigilance of estimable Quakers, who are always ready to denounce to magistrates, those daring infractions of law, and violations of the principles of nature.

At Barbadoes and at Surinam, he who voluntarily and cruelly kills a slave is acquitted of the crime by paying the sum of fifteen pounds sterling to the public treasury.[39] In South Carolina the forfeit is greater: it is there fixed at fifty pounds sterling; but in an American Journal we find that this crime is absolutely committed with impunity, as the sum is never paid.[40]

If the existence of slaves is so precarious, their modesty is surrendered without reserve to all the attacks of brutal lubricity. John Newton, after having been employed nine years in the slave-trade, and who afterwards became an English divine, makes honest minds shudder when he laments the outrages committed against negresses, "although often we must admire traits of modesty and delicacy among them of which a virtuous Englishwoman might be proud."[41]

In the French, English and Dutch colonies, the laws, or public opinion, so prevents marriages between individuals of different colours, that those who would contract them, would be considered as degraded by their alliance. To this prejudice the Portuguese and the Spaniards form an honourable exception, and in their colonies, a catholic marriage is a shield against censure. It is not surprising, that Barre Saint Venant inveighs against this religious regulation,[42] seeing he dares to censure the ever celebrated decree by which Constantine facilitated the enfranchisement of slaves.[43] What has resulted from those prohibitive laws, more particularly those which relate to marriage? Libertinism has eluded or overcome them. This will always take place when men act in contradiction to nature.

I leave to physiologists the task of unfolding the advantages of the mixture of races; with regard to the physical constitution as well as to the energy of the moral faculties, exemplified at the island of St. Helena, where it has produced a magnificent variety of mulattoes. I leave to moralists and politicians, who ought to start from the same principles, but who are often in direct opposition to them, to weigh the consequence of the opinion, which considers it a dishonour to have a negress as a legitimate wife, whilst as a concubine she is no disgrace. Barlow, on the contrary, proposes to encourage mixt marriages by premiums offered for that purpose. Neither the negroes or mulattoes can ever augment the white cast, whilst the latter augments daily that of the mulattoes. The inevitable result will be, that the mulattoes in the end will become masters. Reasoning from this observation, Robin believes, that the distinction of colour is a scourge of colonies, and that St. Domingo would be still in its splendour, if it had followed the Spanish policy, which does not exclude creoles from intermarriage and other social advantages.[44]

The negroes are accused of a vindictive disposition. What other temper can men possess, who are vexed and deceived continually, and even provoked to vengeance. Of this we could cite a thousand proofs; we shall, however, confine ourselves to a single fact. The negro Baron, active, well informed and faithful, is brought to Surinam—in Holland, his master promises him his freedom at his return. Notwithstanding this promise, when he arrived at Surinam, Baron is sold; he obstinately refuses to work; he is lashed at the foot of a gibbet; he escapes, joins the maroons, and becomes the implacable enemy of the whites.

This torturing system has been pursued so far as to prevent the developement of the mental faculties. By a regulation adopted in the state of Virginia, they are not allowed to learn to read. To have been able to read cost one of those black men his life. He demanded, that the Africans should share the benefits which the American liberty promised, and he supported this demand by the first articles of the *bill of rights*. The argument was without reply. In such cases, where refutation is impossible, the inquisition incarcerates those whom formerly it would have burned. All tyrannies have features which resemble each other. The negro suffered on the gallows.

In the government of this lower world, force ought never to intervene except when reason has pleaded in vain. But power generally silences reason. "Is it not shameful to speak as a philosopher, and to act as a despot; to make fine discourses on liberty, and to annex as a commentary, an actual oppression. It is a political maxim that the legislative system ought to harmonize with the principles of the government. Does this harmony exist in a constitution reputed free, if slavery is sanctioned by authority?"

Thus, in 1789, William Pinkney expressed himself, in a discourse delivered before the representative assembly of Maryland, in which sound reasoning is ornamented with erudition and the graces of style, which do equal honour to his heart and his mind.[45]

The employment of executioners was always to calumniate the victims. The merchant Guinea masters and planters have denied, or extenuated the recital of facts of which they have been accused. They have even endeavoured to make a parade of their humanity in supporting the opinion, that all slaves, brought from Africa, were prisoners of war, or criminals destined for punishment, who ought to felicitate themselves that their lives are saved, and that they are permitted to cultivate the soil of the Antilles. They have been refuted by many ocular witnesses, and lately by the honest John Newton, who resided a long time in Africa. He adds, "that the respectable author of the *Spectacle de la Nature,* (Pluche) was led into error in declaring, that fathers sell their children, and children their fathers: I have not heard in Africa that this practice exists there."[46] When the reality of the torture applied to slaves, and the barbarity of their masters have been proven by the most direct evidence, the masters has denied that the negro is susceptible of morality or of intelligence, and have placed him in the scale of beings, between man and the brute.

According to this hypothesis, we may ask, whether man has not rights to exercise and duties to fulfil towards those animals which he associates in labour with himself? and whether he does not offend against religion and morality in overworking those unhappy quadrupeds whose life is nothing more than a continued punishment? Strong maxims on this subject are contained in the sacred books which Christians and Jews equally revere.[47] A bird pursued by a sparrow-hawk seeks refuge in the bosom of the child by whom it is killed. The areopagus condemns it to death. This punishment was doubtless too severe, but will the moment ever arrive when a policy justly rigid will punish those ferocious carters, who daily, more especially at Paris, destroy by fatigue and blows the most useful of all domestic animals— the Horse, which Buffon calls the finest conquest of man. This treatment renders those who practice it, insensible and cruel.

It is with pleasure I recollect to have read at London, at the market of Smithfield, a regulation which imposes a fine on those who abuse animals wantonly.

This discussion is not foreign to my subject, if the principles of morality are applicable to the relations which man has with brutes, the negroes, though deprived of intelligence, have rights to exercise; but if the deepest researches prove, that notwithstanding the different shades of the colour of the skin, whether yellow, copper, black or white, the organization is the same: if the virtues and talents of negroes invincibly demonstrate, that susceptible of all the combinations of intelligence and morals, they constitute, under a different coloured skin, our identical species, how much more guilty do Europeans appear, who, trampling under foot the knowledge and principles propagated, first by christianity, and afterwards by civilization, tear the bodies of unhappy negroes, and suck gold from their blood.

Twenty years of experience have taught me what reply is made by the merchants of human flesh. To understand their reasonings, and to have a right to an opinion on the lawfulness of slavery, a residence in the colonies is necessary, as if the immutable principles of liberty and morality varied according to degrees of latitude. When we offer the irresistible authority of men who have inhabited those climates, and have even been employed in this commerce, they oppose falsehood and calumny. They would finish by slandering *Page,* who after having been one of the most obstinate defenders of slavery, chaunts his recantation, and makes strange avowals, in his work on the restoration of St. Domingo, of which the theme is the freedom of the blacks.[48] The planters obstinately affirm that in colonies, purely agricultural, this first of arts must be tarnished by slavery, as Europeans are unfit for the task. Although this opinion is contradicted by this irrefragable fact, that a colony of Germans was established by Estaing, in 1764, at *Bombade,* near the mole St. Nicholas, whose vigorous inhabitants saw around their habitations a cultivation rich and successful, the fruit of their own labours. Are they ignorant that the first cultivation of the colonial soil was made by whites? In our glass works and foundaries do they not support a heat greater than that of the Antilles? Were it true that these countries cannot flourish without the assistance of negroes, an inference different from that of the colonists would ensue, but they constantly have recourse to the past for the justification of the present, as if inveterate abuses were become legitimate. Do we speak to them of justice? They answer by observations on sugar, indigo, and the balance of commerce. Do we reason with them? They say that we declaim: instead of discussing the subject in their turn, they have recourse to all the false arguments, all the common sayings so often refuted, by which they would support a bad cause. Do we appeal to hearts that can feel? They sneer, and endeavour to carry our views to the poor of the different countries of Europe, to prevent us from fixing them on those unfortunates, whom avarice persecutes in other quarters of the globe, as if the duty of giving to one interdicted us from speaking to others. What idea then do the planters entertain concerning the extent of moral obligations? They pretend that by our love of the human race, we neglect our love of men: because we cannot give comfort to those who surround us but in a manner disproportionate to their number and their wants, we are accused as culpable when we raise our voice in favour of those who, of a different complexion, suffer in distant countries. Such is the author of the voyage in Louisiana.[49] As long as an individual in Europe suffers, these gentlemen would prevent us from lamenting the lot of those, whom they torment in Africa and America. They feel indignant that we trouble the enjoyment of tigers devouring their prey: they have even attempted to vilify the *philanthropist*, or the friend of man, whose pride is to honour him who has not abjured affection for his equals: they have invented the epithets *negrophiles* and *blancophages*, with the hope that they would leave a stain: they have supposed that all the friends of the blacks are in the pay of England, and the enemies of the whites and of France. The author of this work, formerly accused of having received 1,500,000 livres for writing in favour of the Jews, was to receive three millions more for constituting himself the advocate of the negroes. It need not be enquired, why our antagonists have not employed other arms than those of sarcasm and calumny. It is said that a subscription was opened at Nantz, for the purpose of assassinating a *philanthropist*, who had been hung in effigy at Cape François and Jerémi—and this affords an index of what we are to gain when we plead the cause of justice and misfortune.

Frapolosarpi, said with reason, that if the plague had rewards and pensions to bestow, it would find apologists: but in defending the poor and the oppressed, as we must struggle against power, riches and frensy, we may expect nothing but calumny, injuries and persecutions.

The African slave traders have then a bad cause, since it is supported by such means. Let us avenge ourselves by the only means which religion acknowledges. Let us seize every opportunity of doing good to the persecutor, as to him who is persecuted.

Thus have they calumniated negroes, first, in order to have the right to inslave them; and afterwards, in order to justify themselves, because they had enslaved them, and acted culpably towards them. The accusers are both judges and executioners, and they call themselves christians! A thousand times have they attempted to torture the sense of the sacred writings, to find therein an apology for colonial slavery, although the scriptures declare that all are children of the heavenly Father—all mortals are sprung from the same family. Religion admits of no distinction. If, in the churches of the colonies, we sometimes see blacks and those of mulattoes, condemned to places distinct from those of the whites, and even separately admitted to the eucharistical participation, the pastors are criminal in having tolerated an usage so opposed to the spirit of religion. It is particularly in the church, says Paley, where the poor man raises his humiliated form, and where the rich regard him with respect.

It is there, the minister of the altar reminds his auditors of their primitive equality, in the house of a God who declares that with him there is no respect of persons.[50] There the heavenly oracle proclaims that we ought to do to others that which we wish to be done for us.[51]

To the christian religion alone the glory is due of having placed the weak under the protection of the strong. By her influence, in the fourth century, the first hospital was established in the West.[52] She has constantly laboured to console the unhappy, whatever be their country, their colour or religion. The parable of the Samaritan imprints on persecutors the seal of reprobation.[53]

It is an anathema, for ever applied to the person, who would wish to exclude from the circle of his charity a single individual of the human race.

I wish to recal the attention of the reader to a fact attested in history, that the friends of despotism and impiety are always the defenders of slavery, and irreligion, whereas the defenders of the blacks are almost all religious.

The undisputed testimony of protestant authors, among whom is Dallas, reproaches the clergy for neglecting the religious instruction of the negroes, and this inculpation applies to the bishops of London, who have western colonies under their jurisdiction.[54] But these writers bestow eulogiums on catholic missionaries, and on some societies of *dissenters,* such as the Moravians and Quakers, or *Friends,* among whom the love of our neighbour is not a sterile theory. All have discovered an indefatigable zeal to bring the negro slaves to christianity and to freedom. Schools for the education of children of the blacks have been established at Philadelphia and other places by the society of *Friends.* This description of people forms the majority of the committees disseminated over the United States for the abolition of slavery. These committees send deputies to a convention, or central assembly which is held every third year at Philadelphia for the same.[55]

The Quakers, at London, have periodical meetings composed of their representatives, delegated by their brethren of different countries. At the close of the sitting they never fail to terminate their labours by addressing to all those of their profession, a circular letter concerning abuses to be combated, virtues to be practised, and the black slaves are always recommended as fit objects of christian charity.

To Dallas's eulogiums on the catholic priests, he has annexed their correspondence on this subject with the present archbishop of Tours: this prelate with reason remarks, that the circle of their duties is not confined to preaching and reading the liturgy, but that it embraces the care of the sick, the education of children, and visits to families.[56] The catholic religion, more than any other, established various and intimate relations between pastors and those who partake of the sacrament.

An imposing ceremony speaks to the senses, which are, if I may so express myself, the gates of the soul. From these considerations protestant writers acknowledge, and Mackintosh, has repeated to me, that catholic missionaries are much better fitted than those who are not catholics, to make proselytes of negroes, and to afford them consolation.

The first conquerors of America, that they might have a right to butcher the poor Indians, affected to doubt whether they were men. A bull of the Pope destroyed this doubt, and the councils of Mexico present, in this respect, a monument highly honourable to the clergy of those countries. In another work,[57] which I propose to publish, we cannot read, without commiseration the decisions made against negro slavery by the college of Cardinals[58] and that of the Sorbonne.[59]

Elesban, in his calendar of the catholic church, has inserted the names of many blacks. The negroes of the Spanish and Portuguese possessions have adopted this priest as their patron. Under the date of the 27th of October, we may read his life in Baillet, known as a severe critic, but we shall give some details of another black, of whom he has not spoken—a secular brother of the order of recollects.

Benoit of Palermo, also named *Benoit* of St. *Philadelphia,* or of *Santo Fratello; * Benoit the *Moor* and *holy Black,* was the son of a negress slave, and himself a negro. Roccho Pirro, author of the *Sicilia Sacra,* characterizes him by these words: "Nigro quidem corpore sed candore animi præclarisimus quem et miraculis Deus contestatum esse voluit." His body was black, but it pleased God to testify by miracles the whiteness of his soul.[60]

Historians praise in him that assemblage of eminent virtues, which, content to have God only, as a witness, conceal themselves from the sight of man: for real virtues are silent, while vice is noisy: a great crime excites generally more sensation in the world than a thousand good actions. Sometimes nevertheless, whether prompted by justice or by curiosity, men endeavour to remove the modest veil which conceals merit, and it is owing to this, that Benoit the Moor, or the holy Black, has escaped oblivion. He died at Palermo, in 1589, where his tomb and memory are generally revered. This rite, authorised by the Pope, in 1610, and more particularly, in 1743, by a decree of the congregation of church rites, which we may read in Joseph Mary Ancona, the continuator of Wading,[61] will soon obtain more solemnity, if, as had been announced in the Gazettes, at the commencement of this year, they occupy themselves with his canonization. Roccho Pirro, father Arthur,[62] Gravima,[63] and many other writers are full of eulogy concerning the venerable negro, Benoit of Palermo; but in our libraries, altho' very extensive, I have never been able to find his life, neither in Italian, by Tognoletti, nor in Spanish, by Metaplana.

Among the Spaniards and Portuguese, slaves in general have more morality, because they are allowed to partake of the benefits of civilization, and they are not oppressed by labour. Religion continually interposes between them and proprietors, who residing almost always on their plantations, see with their own eyes, and not with those of managers. At Brazil, the curates, appointed by law as the defenders of negroes, can legally force cruel colonists to sell them elsewhere, and the slaves have at least the chance of a better existence.

Among the Spaniards manumissions cannot be refused, on paying a sum fixed by the laws. By habits of economy, the slaves can purchase a day of the week, which facilitates the privilege of a second, of a third, and finally of a whole week, which gives them complete liberty.

In 1765, the English papers, cited as a remarkable event, the ordination of a negro, by Doctor Keppel, bishop of Exeter.[64] Among the Spaniards, and still more among the Portuguese, it is a common occurrence. The history of Congo gives an account of a black bishop who studied at Rome.[65]

The son of a king, and many young people of quality of this country, sent into Portugal, in the time of king Immanuel, were distinguished at the universities, and many of them were promoted to the priesthood.[66]

Near the close of the 17th century, admiral Du Quesne saw, at the isles of Cape Vert, a catholic negro clergy, with the exception of the bishop and curate of St. Yago.[67] In our time, Barrow and Jackquemine Sacré, bishop of Cayenne, found the same establishment still in force.[68]

Laincourt, and a hundred other Europeans, have visited, at Philadelphia, an African church, of which the minister is also a negro.[69]

When we consider, that slavery supposes all the crimes of tyranny, and that it commonly engenders all its vices; that virtue can hardly thrive among men who have no consideration, who are soured by misfortune, dragged into corruption by the example of crimes, driven from all honourable, or supportable ranks in society, deprived of religious and moral instruction, placed in a situation where it is impossible to acquire knowledge, or struggling against obstacles which oppose themselves to the developement of their faculties, we shall find room for surprize, that so many are signalized by estimable qualities. In their place perhaps, we would have been less virtuous, than the virtuous among them, and more vicious than their worst characters. The same reflections apply to the Parias of the Asiatic continent, vilified by the other casts; to Jews of all colours, for there are also blacks of this profession at Cochin, whose history since the dispersion, is nothing but a bloody tragedy; to the Irish catholics, condemned, like the negroes, by a black code, the popery laws. Thus a resemblance offers equally injurious to the inhabitants of Africa and of Ireland, who are represented as hordes of brutes, incapable of self government. The latter like the oppressed of other countries, were to submit irrevocably to the iron sceptre, which, for so many ages, has been kept suspended over them by the English government.[70] This infernal tyranny will exist till an epoch, not far distant, when the brave sons of Erin shall erect the standard of liberty, adopting the sublime invocation of Americans—*an appeal to the justice of Heaven.* Irishmen, Jews and negroes, your talents are yours; your vices are the work of nations called christians.

Notes

1. Considerations on the Negro cause, by Estwick.
2. Modern Colonies under the torrid zone, particularly that of Saint-Domingo, by Barré-St-Venant. 8vo. Paris, 1802. chap. 4.
3. Notes on Virginia, by T. Jefferson, 8vo. London.
4. Topographical description of the western country of North America, by G. Imlay, London, 1793, letter 9th.

5. Topographical description of the western country of North America, by G. Imlay, p. 167.

6. The Guinea Voyage, a Poem in 3 books, by James Field Stanfield, 4to. London, 1789. I beg leave to cite the beginning of the 2d Book.

> High where primeval forests shade the land
> And in majestic solemn order stand,
> A sacred station raises now its seal,
> O'er the loud stream that murmurs at its feet—
> Of Niger rushing thro' the fertile plains,
> Swelled by the Cataract of tropic rains:
> Long ere surcharged, his turged flood divides,
> To burst an ocean in three thundering tides.

7. Long, vol. 2. p. 420.

8. A Provincial Glossary with a collection of local proverbs and popular superstition, by Francis Grose, 8vo. London, 1790.

9. African memoranda, relative to an attempt to establish a British settlement in the island of Boulam, by Capt. Philip Beaver, 4to. London. I would rather carry thither a rattle snake, p. 397.

10. L'aristocratie negriere par l'abbé Sibire, missionaire dans le royaume de Congo, 8vo. Paris, 1789, p. 93.

11. Ibid. p. 27.

12. Practical rules for the management and medical treatment of negro slaves in the sugar colonies, by a professional planter, 8vo. London, 1805, p. 470.

13. Magazin Encyclop. 8vo. London, 1805. p. 470.

14. Voyage to the Island of Madeira, Barbadoes, and Jamaica, by Hans Sloane, 2 vol. fol. London, 1707. p. 43.

15. His Essay against public Slavery, in 1788, Baltimore.

16. Letter of an inhabitant of Martinique to Mr. Petit, on his work entitled, The public right of government over the French colonies, 8vo. 1778.

17. Voyage to Cochin China, by Barrow, v. II. p. 98, 99.

18. Voyage à lîle du Ceylan, by Robert Percival, translated by P.F. Henry, 1803.

19. Qui se læsum clamabit is conscientiam suam prodet.

20. Thoughts on the African slave-trade, by John Newton, 2d edit. 8vo. London, 1798, p. 17 and 18.

21. American Museum, 8vo. Philadelphia, 1789, v. VI. p. 407.

22. See the horrible details of this in Dallas, vol. II. letter 9. p. 4, &c.

23. Voyage to the West-Indies, by Bossu, 1769, Amsterdam, 1769, p. 14.

24. The horror of the negro slavery existing in our West-Indian islands, irrefragably demonstrated from official documents recently presented to the house of commons, 8vo. London, 1805.

25. Notes on the West-Indies, by G. Pinckard.

26. Voyage dans l'interieur de la Louisiane, de la Floride, &c. par Robin, 3 vols. 8vo. Paris, 1807.

27. Vol. I. p. 175, and following.

28. Dissertation on the question, whether it is permitted to have slaves, &c. in the colonies of America, by P. Fermin, 8vo. Mastrich, 1776.

29. Will. Beckford, 2 vols. 8vo. London, 1790, vol. II. p. 382.

30. Considerations on the present state of St. Domingo, by H.D.L. Hilliard D'Auberteuil, 8vo. Paris, 1777, p. 73. and following.

31. Evenings in Burmuda, concerning the events which have operated the ruin of the French part of St. Domingo, by F.C. one of its former colonists, Bordeaux, 1802, p. 60. and 66.

32. Voyage in Louisiana, and on the continent of America, by B.D. 8vo. Paris, 1802, p. 147. and 191.

33. Examination, &c. by V. D. C. formerly lawyer at St. Domingo, 2 vols. 8vo. Paris, 1802.

34. See p. 22.

35. Ibid. p. 110.

36. Ibid. p. 102.

37. Ibid. p. 102.

38. Long, Vol. 2. p. 489.

39. Remarks on the slave trade, 4to. 1788, p. 125.

40. Literary Magazine and American Register, 8vo. Philadelphia, 1803. p. 36.

41. Thoughts upon slavery, p. 20, and following.

42. Barre St. Venant, p. 92.

43. Ibid. p. 120 and 121.

44. Vol. I. p. 281.

45. American Museum, or Annual Register for the year 1778, 8vo. Philadelphia, p. 79, and following.

46. Ibid. p. 31.

47. Deut. xxvi. 6. I Tim. 13. Non alligabis, &c.

48. Treatise on the political economy of the colonies, by Page, 1st part, 8vo. Paris, year 7. 2d part, year 10.

49. P. 103, and following. It is, I believe, Berquin Duvallon.

50. II. Paral. 19.7. Eccles. 20.24. Rom. 2. 11. Ephés. 6.9. Coloss. 3.25. James 2.1. 1st Peter 1.13.

51. Matthew 7.12.

52. Memoir on different subjects of literature, by Monges, Paris, 1780, p. 14. and Commentatio de vi quam religio christiana habuit, by Paetz, 4to. Goetting, 1799.

53. The colonists and their friends are in the habit of repeating accusations of which the absurdity has been demonstrated in a manner that admits of no reply: thus Dupont, author of the Voyage in *Terra Firma,* vol I. p. 308. mentions that Las Casas, Bishop of Chiappo, has usurped the honours of celebrity, and voted for the slavery of negroes. It is now six years since my apology of Las Casas was printed in a volume of the Memoirs of the National Institute, class of moral and political sciences, p. 44. We refer Dupont to this paper, and invite a reply. The author of the voyage in Louisiana, Berquin Duvallon, again presents the same imposture, p. 105, and following.

54. Dallas, vol. II. p. 427, and following.

55. I seize with pleasure this occasion of expressing my gratitude, 1st. To the presidents and secretaries of these conventions, who, during many years, has sent

me the minutes of their proceedings; and 2d, To Mr. Philips, a Quaker, and a Bookseller at London, who, during my stay in England, procured me many rare and useful works on the freedom of the blacks.

56. Ibid. p. 430, and following.

57. History of the liberty of negroes, read at the settings of the class of moral and political science of the National Institute.

58. In the collection of voyages of Astley, vol. II, p. 154. and Benezet, p. 50.

59. Labat, vol. IV, p. 120.

60. Sicilia sacra, &c. auctore don. Roccho Pirro, 3d ed.

61. Annales minorum, &c. continuati—Maria di Ancona, fol. May 20, 1745, vol. XIX, p. 201 & 202.

62. Martyrologium franciscanum cura et labore, fol. Paris, 1638, p. 32.

63. Vox turturis seu de florenti adusque nostra tempora sanctorum Benedicti, dominici francisci. &c.

64. Gentleman's Magazine, 35th year, 1765, p. 145.

65. Prevot, General History of voyages, vol. V. p. 53.

66. History of Portugal, by Clede, 2 vol. 4to. Paris, 1735, vol. I. p. 594, 95.

67. Journal of a voyage to the East Indies, on board the squadron of Du Quesne, 2 vol. in 12mo. Rouen, 1721, vol. I. p. 193, and narrative of a voyage to and return from the East Indies, during the years 1690, and 1691, by Claude Michel Ponchot de Chantassin, of the guard on board De Quesne, &c. 12mo. Paris, p. 80.

68. Barrow. Voyage to Cochin China, 1 vol. p. 87.

69. Voyage in the United States of America, by Rochefoueaut Laincourt, 8vo. Paris, year 8. vol. VI. p. 334.

70. In "*Pieces of Irish History,*" an interesting work, published by McNeven, 8vo. New-York, 1807. There is a precious narrative by Emmet, his friend, entitled, "*Part of an essay towards the History of Ireland.*"

Chapter III

Moral qualities of the negroes; their love of industry, courage,
bravery, paternal tenderness, filial generosity, &c.

The introductory remarks we have read are not foreign to my subject. I could have hastily approached the question, and shewn, by a multitude of facts, the aptitude of the negroes for virtue and talents. Facts are the best reply.

The negroes are accused of idleness. Bosman, to prove it, says that they are in the habit of asking, not, How do you do? but, How have you reposed?[1] The maxim with them is, that it is better to be lying than seated: better to be seated than to stand, and better to stand than to walk. Since we made them so wretched, they have added this Indian proverb, that death is preferable to all this.

The accusation of indolence, which is not without some degree of truth, is often exaggerated. It is exaggerated in the mouth of those who are accustomed to employ a bloody whip to conduct slaves to forced labour; it is true that in this situation men cannot have a great inclination to industry, either, when they have no property, not even that of their own person, and when the fruits of their sweat feed the luxury or avarice of a merciless master; or, when in countries favoured by nature, her spontaneous productions, or an easy industry, abundantly supply wants which are merely natural. But blacks or whites, all are laborious when stimulated by the spirit of property, by utility, or by pleasure. Such are the negroes of Senegal, who work with ardour, says

Pelletan, because they are unmolested in their possessions and enjoyments. Since the suppression of slavery, adds he, the Moors make no more inroads upon them—thus villages are rebuilt and repeopled.[2]

Such are the laborious inhabitants of Axiam on the golden coast, whom all travellers love to describe.[3] The negroes of the country of Boulam, whom Beaver mentions as innured to industry;[4] those of the country of Jagro, celebrated for an activity which enriches their country;[5] those of Cabomonte and of Fido or Juido, are infatigable cultivators, says Bosman, who certainly is not prejudiced in their favour; economical of their soil, they scarcely leave a foot path to form a communication between the different possessions; they reap one day, and the next, they sow the same earth, without allowing it time for repose.[6] They are too sensible of the allurements of pleasure to resist them often; they know however, how to support pain with a courage truly heroic, and which perhaps, must be partly attributed to their athletic constitution. History is full of traits of their intrepidity. Punishments of the most horrible description, multiplied by the cruelty of the whites, have afforded proofs of this. Can life be desirable, when existence itself is a perpetual calamity? Slaves have been seen, after many days of uninterrupted torture, and almost in the grasp of death, to converse calmly among themselves, and even to smile at torture.[7]

A negro at Martinico, condemned to be burned, and passionately fond of tobacco, begged to have a lighted cigar, which was put in his mouth: he continued to smoke, says Labat, even when his members, were attacked by the fire.

In 1750, the negroes of Jamaica revolted, with Tucky as their chief: their tyrants remaining conquerors condemned many to the fire, and all marched gaily to punishment; one, without emotion saw his limbs reduced to ashes—one hand was disengaged, the flame having consumed the cord which confined it, he seizes a brand, and darts it against the face of the executioner.[8]

In the seventeenth century, when Jamaica was still under the dominion of the Spaniards, a party of slaves, under the command of John de Bolas, regained their independence. They increased in numbers and became formidable after they had elected Cudjoe, as chief, whose portrait is seen in Dallas's work. Cudjoe, equally brave, skillful and enterprising, in 1730, established a confederation among all the Maroon tribes, made the English tremble, and compelled them to make a treaty, in which they acknowledged the freedom of the blacks, and they ceded to them for ever a portion of the territory of Jamaica.[9]

The Portuguese historian Borros, says, in some part of his work, that the negroes were in his opinion, preferable to Swiss soldiers. To heighten the praises of the former, a comparison was made with the Helvetians, which he considered as the most honourable. Among the traits of bravery which Labat has collected, one of the most remarkable happened at the seige of Carthagena: all the troops of the line had been repulsed at the attack of fort Bochachique. The negroes, brought from St. Domingo, attacked with such impetuosity that the beseiged were forced to surrender.[10]

In 1703, the blacks took arms for the defence of Guadaloupe, and were more useful than all the rest of the French troops, at the same time, they defended Martinico against the English.[11] The honourable conduct of the negroes and mulattoes, at the siege of Savannah, at the taking of Pensecola, is well known; and also during our revolution, when incorporated with the French troops, they shared their dangers and their glory.

The African prince Oronoko, sold at Surinam, was a negro. Madam Behu had been a witness of his misfortunes. She had seen the fidelity and courage of the negroes contrasted with the baseness and perfidy of their tyrants. Having returned to England she composed her *Oronoko*. It is to be regretted that on a historical canvas she has painted a romance. The simple recital of the misfortunes of this new Spartacus was sufficient to interest the reader.

Henry Diaz, who is extolled in all the histories of Brasil, was a negro. Once a slave, he became colonel of a regiment of foot-soldiers of his own colour, to whom Brandano (who was certainly not a colonist) bestows the praise of talents and sagacity. This regiment, composed of blacks, still exists in Portuguese America, under the name of *Henry Diaz*. The Hollanders, then possessors of Brasil, disturbed its inhabitants. This circumstance gives La Clede occasion to reflect on the impolicy of conquerors, who, instead of conciliation, aggravate their yoke, and foster hatreds, which sooner or later, have a reaction cruel to tyrants and useful to the liberty of the people. In 1637, Henry Diaz, in order to chase away the Hollanders, joined the Portuguese. The former, being beseiged in the town of Arecise, having made a sally, were repulsed with great loss, by a negro general. He took the fort by assault which they had erected at some distance from this town. To a knowledge of military tactics and warlike manœvre, by which the

Dutch generals were often disconcerted, they combined the most determined courage. In a battle, struggling against a superiority of numbers,
and perceiving that some of his soldiers began to give way, he darts
into the midst of them, crying, *are these the brave companions of
Henry Diaz?* His discourse and his example, says a historian, gives
them fresh courage, and the enemy, who already thought itself victorious, is attacked with an impetuosity which obliges it to fall back pre-
cipitately into the town. Henry Diaz forces Arecise to capitulate,
Fernanbon to surrender, and entirely destroys the Batavian army.

In 1745, in the midst of his exploits, a ball pierced his left hand; to
spare the delay of dressing the wound, he caused it to be amputated,
saying, that each finger of his right is worth a hand in combat. It is to
be regretted, that history does not inform us where, when, and how this
general died. Menezes praises his consummate experience, and speaks of
the Africans, who all of a sudden are converted into intrepid warriors.[12]

The unfortunate Oge, worthy of a better fate, was a man of colour.
He sacrificed himself to insure his mulatto brethren and free negroes,
all the advantages which they might anticipate, from the decree of the
Constituent Assembly, of the fifteenth of May; a decree which, without
asperity, would have gradually introduced into the colonies, an order
of things conformable to justice. Enraged at the perversity of the colonists; who not only prevented the execution of laws, but who found
means to induce the government to prevent the embarkation of negroes
and mulattoes, he forms the resolution to return to the Antilles. The
author of this work, so often accused for having advised him to depart,
in vain represents to him that he must temporize, and not compromit,
by a precipitate conduct, the success of so just a cause. Notwithstanding his advice, Oge found means in 1791, of repassing, by the way of
England and the American continent, to St. Domingo. He demands the
execution of the decrees. His reclamation founded upon reason, and
sanctioned by divine authority, is rejected. The parties are exasperated,
and an attack ensues. Oge is perfidiously delivered up by the Spanish
government. His process discloses a secret well known in the tribunals of
the Inquisition; he demands a defender; his request is refused: thirteen of
his companions are condemned to the galleys, more than twenty to the
gibbet, and Oge with Chavanne are destined to the torture of the wheel.
They carry their animosity so far as to make a distinction between the
place of punishment for the mulattoes and for the whites. In a report in
which these facts are examined with impartiality, Garran, after having

justified Oge, concludes with these words: "We cannot refuse a tear to his ashes, but leave his executioners to the judgment of history."[13]

Saint George, called the Voltaire of equitation, of fencing and instrumental music, was a man of colour. By the *amateurs* of these exercises he was placed in the first rank, and by compositors, in the second, or third. Some of his *concertos* are still held in estimation. Although he was a hero in gymnastics, yet it is difficult to believe, with his admirers, that he could with a gun fire at, and strike a ball projected in the air.

According to the traveller Arndt, this new Alcibiades was the finest, strongest, and most amiable of his contemporaries; and besides, he was generous, a good citizen, and a good friend.[14] All people of fashion, or, in other words, frivolous people, considered him as an accomplished man. He was the idol of fashionable societies.

When he fought with the Chevalier D'Eon, it was almost an affair of state, because then the state was nothing for the public. When St. George, who was considered as the best swordsman of his time, was to fence, or to exhibit his musical talents, the newspaper announced it to the idle of the capital. His bow and his foil set all Paris in motion. Thus formerly they assembled at Seville when a brotherhood of negroes which had not been destroyed, but, which for want of subjects, exists no more, formed on certain holy days, brilliant processions, and performed various manœuvres and evolutions.[15]

I do not think, as Malherbes, that a good player at nine pins is of as great importance as a good poet; but are all the amiable talents united, worth one that is really useful? What pity that the happy inclinations of St. George had not been directed towards pursuits which would have procured him the esteem and gratitude of his fellow citizens? We may however recollect, that enlisted under the banners of the republic be served in the war of freedom.

Alexander Dumas was a mulatto, who, with four men, near Lisle, attacked a post of fifty Austrians, killed six, and made sixteen prisoners. He, during a long time, commanded a legion of horse, composed of blacks and mulattoes, who were the terror of their enemies.

In the army of the Alps, with charged bayonet, he ascended St. Bernard, defended by a number of redoubts, and took possession of the cannon, which he immediately directed against the enemy. Others have already recounted the exploits by which he signalized himself in Europe and in Africa, for he belonged to the expedition of Egypt; on his return he had the misfortune to fall into the hands of the Neapolitan government, who kept him and Dolomieu two years in irons. Alexander Dumas, General of Division, named by Bonaparte, the Horatius Coeles of the Tyrols, died in 1807.

John Kina, of St. Domingo, was a negro, he was a partizan of a bad cause, for he fought against the blacks, but his valour gained him the most flattering reception at London. The British government confided to him the command of a company of men of colour, destined to protect the remote quarters of the colony of Surinam. In 1800, he crossed over the Antilles: a humiliating pride reminds him that he is free; his heart swells with this sensation. He excites an insurrection to protect his brethren against the colonists, who, by employing the negresses in hard labour, caused them to miscarry; and who resolved to expose free negroes to sale. He is soon apprehended, sent to London, and shut up in Newgate.[16]

Mentor, born at Martinico, in 1771, was a negro. In fighting against the English he was made prisoner. In sight of the coast of Ushant, he took possession of the vessel which was conducting him to England, and carried her into Brest. To a noble physiognomy he united an amenity of character, and a mind improved by culture. We have seen him occupy the legislative seat at the side of the estimable Tomany. Such was Mentor, whose latter conduct has perhaps sullied these brilliant qualities. He was killed at St. Domingo.

Toussaint Louverture had worn the chains of slavery, for he had been a herdsman at the plantation of Breda, to the Intendant of which, he sent pecuniary aid, who, with Reymond, the mulatto, associate of the National Institute, formed a democratic constitution for St. Domingo. His bravery and that of Rigaud, a mulatto general, and his competitor cannot be contested, for it had been displayed on many occasions. In this view he resembles the Cacique Henry, whose memory Charlevoix has celebrated.

I have seen a very curious manuscript, entitled, *Reflections on the present state of the colony of St. Domingo, by Vincent, engineer.* The following is the portrait he presents of the negro general.

"Toussaint, at the head of his army, is the most active and indefatigable man of whom we can form an idea, we may say, with truth, that he is found wherever instructions or danger render his presence necessary. The particular care which he employs in his march, of always deceiving the men of whom he has need, and who think they enjoy a

confidence he gives to none, has such an effect, that he is daily expected in all the chief places of the colony. His great sobriety, the
faculty, which none but he possesses, of never reposing, the facility
with which he resumes the affairs of the cabinet after the most tire-
some excursions, of answering daily a hundred letters, and of habitu-
ally tiring five secretaries, render him so superior to all those around
him, that their respect and submission are in most individuals carried
even to fanaticism. It is certain that no man, in the present times, has
obtained such an influence over a mass of ignorant people, as general
Toussaint possesses over his brethren in St. Domingo."

Vincent, the engineer adds, that Toussaint is endowed with a prodi-
gious memory; that he is a good father, a good husband, and that his
civil qualities are as solid, as his political life is cunning and culpable.

Toussaint re-established religious worship at Śt. Domingo, and on
account of his zeal in this respect he was named the *capuchine,* by a
class of men who certainly merited the name of persecutors. With
myself, he had a curious correspondence, the object of which was to
obtain, twelve ecclesiastics. Several set out for that island, under the
direction of the estimable bishop Mauviel Sacré, for St. Domingo, who
generously devoted himself to this painful mission. Toussaint, had con-
gratulated the colony on his arrival, by a solemn proclamation, yet
afterwards led astray by the suggestion of some monks, the bishop
experienced difficulties. That Toussaint may have been cruel, hypocriti-
cal, and deceitful, as well as the negroes and mulattoes who accompanied
his operations, I do not pretend either to affirm, nor to deny; for we do not
judge a cause from the hearing of one party only. Some day, perhaps, the
negroes will write and print in their turn, or the pen of some white may be
guided by truth. Recent facts, it is observed, are under the dominion of
adulation, or of satire. Whilst among us the negro general is painted in
the most odious colours: Whitchurch, in his poem, pursuing another
extreme, has made him a hero.[17] Though Toussaint is dead, posterity,
which destroys, confirms, or rectifies the judgments of contemporaries,
has not yet passed sentence on his character.

Notes

1. Voyage in Guinea, by Bosman, Utrecht, 1705, p. 131.
2. Memoirs on the French colony of Senegal, by Pelletan, 8vo. Paris, years 9,
p. 69. &c.

3. Prevot, vol. IV. p. 117.
4. Beaver, p. 383.
5. Ledyard, vol. II. p. 332.
6. Labat, vol. IV. p. 183.
7. Labat, vol. IV. p. 183.
8. Bryant Edwards's history of the West-Indies, and the Bibliotheque Brittanique, vol. IX, p. 495, and following.
9. Dallas, vol. I p. 25, 46, 60, &c.
10. Labat, vol. IV. p. 184.
11. Memoir of the king against Poupet, by Poucet de la Grave Henrion de Poucet et de Fois, 8vo. Paris, 1770, p. 14.
12. Nova Lusitania, istoria de guerras Brasiliças, by Francisco de Brito Freyre, folio, Lisbon, 1675, B. VIII, p 610; and B. IX, No. 762. Istoria delle guerre di Portogallo, &c. di Alessandro Brandano, 4to. Venezia, 1689, p. 181, 329, 364, 393, &c.

Istoria delle guerre del regno del Brasile, &c. dal P.F.G. Jioseppe, di santa Theresa Carmelitano, folio, Roma, 1698, parte I, p. 133 and 183; part II, p. 103, and following.

Historiarum Lusitanarum libri, &c. autore Fernando de Menezes, comite Ericeyra, 2 vols. 4to. Ulyssippone, 1734, p. 606, 635, 675. &c. La Clede, histoire de Portugal, &c. Passim.

13. Report on the troubles of St. Domingo, by Garranto. Paris, year 6, vol. II, p. 52, and following, p. 78.
14. Bruch-Stücke einer reise durch Frankreich im frühling and sommer, 1799, von *Ernst Moritz Arndt,* 3 vol. 8vo. Leipzi, 1802, vol. II, p. 36 and 37.
15. Note communicated by Mr. de Lasteyric, who has made several scientific voyages in Spain, the publication of which is expected. The work will justify the hopes of the public.
16. Work entitled, Paris, vol. XXXI, p. 405, &c.
17. Hispaniola, a Poem, by Samuel Whitchurch, 12mo. London, 1805.

Chapter IV

Continuation of the same Subject.

Nobleness of character is the inseparable companion of true bravery. The facts which are now to be narrated, will in this respect, place the blacks and whites on a parallel. The impartial reader will hold the balance.

The negro Maroons of Jacmel have been, for almost a century, the terror of St. Domingo. Bellecombe, the most imperious of governors, in 1785, was by them obliged to capitulate. There were not more than one hundred and twenty-five men on the French side, and five on the Spanish. It is Page, the planter, who asks,[1] has it ever been heard that those men violated the capitulation; although they were, like wolves, chased from the bushes?

In 1718, when we were in peace with the red Caribs of St. Vincent, who are known to carry their bravery even to rashness, and who are more active and industrious than the white Caribs, an unjust and unsuccessful expedition was directed against those of Martinico. Instead of being irritated, the year following they mildly acquiesced in a peace; these traits, says Chauvelin, are not found in the history of civilized nations.[2]

In 1726, the Maroons of Surinam, whom the ferocity of the colonists had driven to despair, obtained their liberty with the sword and forced their oppressors to a treaty; they religiously observed their conventions. Do the colonists merit the same praise? They, willing to negotiate a peace, ask a conference with the negroes: this is granted, and as a preliminary it is stipulated, that with many useful objects, they should send them good fire-arms and ammunition.

Two Dutch commissaries under escort, appear in the camp of the negroes. Captain Boston, their commander, perceives that the commissaries bring only trifles, scissars, combs and small mirrors, and neither fire-arms nor powder; with a voice of thunder he addresses them: "Do Europeans think that negroes have need only of combs and scissars? One of such articles is sufficient for us all; one barrel of powder would have testified that the Hollanders have confidence in us."

The negroes, however, instead of yielding to a sentiment of just indignation against a government which broke its engagements, give a year to deliberation, and to choose either peace or war. They honor the commissaries with *fetes,* treat them with the most generous hospitality, and in parting, remind them that the colonists of Surinam, by their inhumanity to their slaves, were themselves the authors of their own misfortunes.[3] Stedman, to whom we owe these details, adds, that the fields of this republic of blacks were covered with maize, *Ignames plantanier manioc.*

All unprejudiced authors, who speak of negroes, do justice to their natural disposition and virtues. Some even of those, who are the partizans of slavery, are occasionally compelled by truth to make avowals in their favour. Such are, 1st, Long, the historian of Jamaica, who found some of excellent character, good and grateful, and remarkable for paternal and filial tenderness.[4] 2d, Duvallon, whose recital of the misfortunes of the poor and decrepid Irrouba, cannot fail to move the heart of the reader, and force him to execrate the ferocious colonist, of whom she had been the foster mother.[5]

The same virtues of negroes are conspicuous, in the narrative, by Hilliard D'Auberteuil, Falconbridge, Grandville, Sharp, Benezet, Ramsay, Horneman, Pinkard, Robin, and particularly my excellent friend Clarkson, who, as well as Wilberforce, is immortalized by his works and his zeal in the defence of Africans. George Roberts, an English navigator, pillaged by the captain of a privateer belonging to his country, sought refuge in the isle of St. John, in the Archipelago, near Cape Vert. The negroes give him succour. An anonymous pamphleteer, who dare not deny the fact, endeavours to extenuate its merit, in saying that the condition of George Roberts would have moved a tyger to pity.[6] Durand extols the modesty and chastity of negroe wives, and the good education of the mulattoes at Goree.[7] Wadstrom, who boasts much of their friendship, thinks their sensibility more mild and affecting than that of the whites. Captain Wilson, who lived among them, speaks highly of their constancy in friendship: they shed tears at his departure.

Some negroes of St. Domingo, had from attachment, followed their masters to Louisiana, who sold them there. This, and the following fact, taken from Robin, furnish materials for a moral comparison between the blacks and the whites. A slave had runaway; the master promised a reward of twelve dollars to him who brought him back; he is conducted to the master by a negro, who refuses to accept the reward; he only asks pardon for the deserter, the master grants it, and keeps the sum he offered. The author of the voyage remarks, that the master had the soul of a slave, and the slave that of a master.[8]

Doctor Newton relates that one day he accused a negro of imposture and injustice. The latter, with pride, replies, do you take me for a white?[9] He adds, that on the borders of the river Gabaon, the negroes are the best race of men that exists.[10] Ledyard says the same of the Foulahs, whose government is paternal.[11]

Proyart, in his history of Loango asserts, that if the negroes, who inhabit its coasts, and who associate with Europeans, are inclined to fraud and libertinism; those of the interior are humane, obliging, and hospitable.[12] This eulogium is repeated by Golberry: he inveighs against the presumption with which Europeans despise and calumniate nations, improperly called savage, among whom we find men of probity, models of filial, conjugal and paternal affection, who know all the energies and refinements of virtue, among whom sentimental impressions are more deep, because they observe, more than we, the dictates of nature, and know how to sacrifice personal interest to the ties of friendship. Golberry furnishes many proofs of this.[13]

The anonymous author of the *West Indian Eclogues,*[14] owes his life to a negro, who, to save it, sacrificed his own. Why has not this poet, who, in a note relates this circumstance, mentioned the name of his preserver!

Adamson, who visited Senegal, in 1754, and who describes this country as an Elysium, found the negroes very sociable, obliging, humane and hospitable: their amiable simplicity, says he, in this enchanting country, recalled to me the idea of the primitive race of man: I thought I saw the world in its infancy. They have generally preserved an estimable simplicity of domestic manners. They are distinguish—by their tenderness for their parents, and great respect for the aged—a patriarchal virtue, which, in our days, is almost unknown.[15]

Those who are Mahometans contract a particular alliance with those who are circumcised at the same epoch, and consider them as brethren during the rest of their lives. Those who are christians always preserve a particular veneration for their god-fathers and god-mothers. These words recal to mind a sublime institution of which philosophy in latter times might envy christianity—this kind of religious adoption connects children by certain ties of love and kindness, that in the event of the death of their parents, which unfortunately happens too often, prepare for orphans, advice and an asylum.

Robin speaks of a slave of Martinico, who having gained money sufficient for his own ransom, purchased with it his mother's freedom. The most horrible outrage that can be committed against a negro, is to curse his father or his mother,[16] or to speak of either with contempt. Strike me, said a slave to his master, but curse not my mother.[17] It is from Mungo Park, I take this, and the following fact. A negress having lost her son, her only consolation was, that he had never told a lie.[18] Casaux ralates, that a negro seeing a white man abuse his father, said, carry away the child of this monster that it may not learn to imitate his conduct.

The veneration of blacks for their grandfather or grandmother is not confined to life: in mournful sympathy they hang over the ashes of those who are no more. A traveller has preserved the anecdote of an African who recommended a Frenchman to respect places of interment. What would the African have thought, if he could have believed that one day they would be profaned throughout all France—a nation which boasts of its civilization.

The blacks, according to the account of Stedman, are so benevolent one to another, that it is useless to say to them, love your neighbour as yourself.[19] Slaves, particularly those of the same country, have a decided inclination to assist each other. Alas! it happens always, that the wretched have nothing to hope but from their associates in misfortune.

Several maroons had been condemned to the gallows: one has the offer of his life, provided he becomes the executioner of his fellows: he refuses: he prefers death. The master orders one of his negroes to perform this office. Wait, said he, till I get ready, he goes into the house, takes a hatchet, cuts off his hand, returns to his master, and says to him; order me now to be the executioner of my comrade.[20]

We are indebted to Dickson for the following fact. A negro had killed a white man: another accused of the crime was about to suffer death. The murderer acknowledged his crime, because, said he, "I cannot suffer the remorse I must feel from the idea of being the cause of the death of two individuals. The innocent man is released; the negro is sent to the gibbet, where he remained alive during six or seven days.

The same Dickson has informed us that among one hundred and twenty thousand negroes and creoles of Barbadoes, only three murders have been known to be committed by them in the course of thirty years, although often provoked by the cruelty of the planters.[21] I doubt whether an inspection of the criminal tribunals of Europe would give a like result.

The gratitude of the blacks, says Stedman, is such, that they often expose their life to save that of their benefactor.[22] Cowry relates, that a Portuguese slave having fled to the woods, learns that his master is brought to trial for the crime of assassination: the negro goes to prison instead of his master, gives false, though judiciary proofs of his pretended crime, and suffers death instead of the criminal.[23]

The anecdote of Louis Desrouleaux, a negro pastry cook, of Nantes, is little known. After he left Nantes, he lived at the Cape, where he had been a slave of Pinsum, of Bayonne, a captain in the negro trade, who came with great riches to France, where he was at last ruined. He returns to St. Domingo. Those who, when he was rich, called themselves his friends, now scarcely recognized him. L. Desrouleaux, who had acquired a fortune, supplies their place. He learns the misfortune of his old master, hastens to find him, gives him lodging and nourishment, and nevertheless proposes that he should live in France, where his feelings will not be mortified by the sight of ungrateful men. But I cannot find a subsistance in France—will an annual revenue of fifteen thousand francs be sufficient—The colonist weeps with joy. The negro signs the contract, and the pension was regularly paid, till the death of Louis Desrouleaux, which happened in 1774.

If it were permitted to insert a fact foreign to my subject, I would cite the conduct of the Indians towards the Bishop Jacqumin, who was twenty-two years a missionary, at Guyanne. These Indians, who loved him tenderly, seeing him stripped of all, at the time when they had ceased to employ Pastors, went to him, and said; Father, thou art aged: remain with us; we will hunt and fish for thee.

And how can these sons of nature be ungrateful to their benefactors, when they are generous even to their tyrants at sea? The blacks in chains, have been seen to share, with the sailors their unwholesome and scanty nourishment.[24]

A contagious disease had carried off the captain, the mate, and most of the sailors of a vessel in the negro trade: those who remained were incapable of conducting the vessel: the negroes assist; and by their aid the vessel arrives at her destined port, where the slaves suffer themselves to be sold.[25]

The philanthropists of England, take a pleasure in speaking of the good and religious Joseph Rachel, a free negro, of Barbadoes, who, having become rich by commerce, consecrated all his fortune to acts of charity and beneficence. The unfortunate, whatever was his colour, had a claim upon his affections. He gave to the indigent, lent to those who could not make a return, visited prisoners, gave them good advice; and endeavoured to bring back the guilty to virtue. He died, at Bridgetown, in 1758, equally lamented by blacks and whites.[26]

The French ought to bless the memory of Jasmin Thoumazeau, born in Africa, in 1714. He was sold at St. Domingo, in 1736. Having obtained his freedom, he married a negress of the Golden coast, and, in 1756, established a hospital, at the Cape, for poor negroes and mulattoes. During more than forty years, he and his wife, were occupied in giving them comfort, and rendering his fortune subservient to their wants. The only pain they felt, in the midst of those unfortunates, who were solaced by their charity, arose from the idea, that after their death, the hospital might be abandoned. The Philadelphian society at the Cape, and the agricultural society at Paris, decreed medals to Jasmin,[27] who died near the close of the century.

Moreau St. Mery, and many other writers inform us, that negresses and female mulattoes discover great maternal tenderness and charity for the poor.[28] Proofs of this are found in an anecdote which has not yet received all the publicity it merits. Mungo Park, in the bosom of Africa, was ready to perish by hunger. A good negress meets him, conducts him to her hut, treats him in the most hospitable manner, assembles the women of the family, who passed a part of the night spinning cotton, and singing extemporary songs to amuse the *white man,* whose appearance in that country was an enticing novelty. He was the subject of one of these songs, which brings to mind the idea of Hervey in his *meditations.* I think I hear the winds plead the cause of the wretched.[29] It is as follows:—"The winds howled, and the rain fell: the poor white man, weary with fatigue, sits down under our tree: he has no mother to bring him milk, no woman to grind his corn;" the other women sang in chorus: "pity the poor white man, he has no mother to bring him milk, no woman to grind his corn."[30]

Such are the men calumniated by Descroizilles, who, in 1803, published a treatise, in which he asserts that social affections and religious institutions have taken no hold on this character.[31]

To those traits of virtue practised by negroes, and to the honourable testimony which authors have rendered them, I might have added many others which may be found in the official depositions made at the bar of the Parliament of England.[32] That which we have read will suffice to avenge offended truth and insulted humanity.

Let us, however, guard against the extravagant exaggeration, that among blacks we find none but estimable qualities: but we whites, have we the right to constitute ourselves their denunciators? Persuaded that we can but rarely depend on the virtue and integrity of men, of any colour, I have tried to prove that one race is not originally inferior to the other.

It is an error almost general to call those individuals virtuous, who have only, if I may so express myself, a negative morality. Their character is not decided—they are incapable of thinking or of acting for themselves; they have neither the courage of virtue, nor the boldness of vice: equally susceptible of good, or of bad impressions, their ideas and inclinations are all borrowed: what in them is called goodness and mildness is really nothing but apathy, weakness and dulness. It is this description of persons that gave rise to the proverb: *There are individuals so good that they are worth nothing.*

In the picture of important facts here presented, we, on the contrary, find *that* energy *(vis virtus,)* which makes sacrifices for the good of others, and obliges men to act conformably to the principles of morality. This practical reason, the fruit of a cultivated understanding, manifests itself also under other vices, although, among most negroes, civilization and the arts are still in their infancy.

Notes

1. Treatise on the political economy and commerce of the colonies.
2. Voyage in Martinico, by Chauvelin, 4to. p. 39, and following.

3. Stedman, vol. I. p. 88, and following.

4. Long, vol. II, p. 416.

5. View of the Spanish colony, in 1802, by Duvallon, 8vo. Paris, 1803, p. 268, and the following. "Let us visit the old woman, who has seen her hundredth year, says some one of the company; and we advanced to the door of a little hut, where an old negress of Senegal appeared, and so decrepitated, that she was bent towards the ground, and obliged to lean against the side of her hut to receive the company assembled at the door: she was also deaf, but her eye was still lively. Every thing around her shewed that she was destitute and wretched. She had scarcely rags enough to cover her nakedness, and had not brands sufficient to give warmth, at a season when the cold is as sensibly felt by the old, and more particularly by those of the black race. We found her occupied in boiling a little water and rice for her supper. For she received not from her master that regular subsistance which her great age and former services required. She was besides, alone and abandoned, her strength exhausted and more indebted to nature than to them. The reader ought to know that independently of her long services, this woman, now in her hundredth year, had formerly nourished, with her milk, two white children, whom she had seen arrive at complete growth, and whom she afterwards accompanied to the tomb; and these were the brothers of one of the masters then present.—The old woman perceived him, and called him by his name, and *tutagant* him (according to the custom of the negroes of Guinea) with an air of kindness truly affecting, and when, said she, wilt thou repair the roof of my hut? It was almost uncovered, and the rain poured freely. The master raised his eye towards it; it was no higher than the hand could reach; I shall think of this, said he. Thee will think of it, thee always tells me so, but nothing is ever done. Hast thee not thy children (two negroes of the work shop, her grand-children) who could mend the hut; and thee, art thee not their master, and art thee not thyself my son? Come, said she, taking him by the arm, and introducing him into the Cabin, come and see thyself these openings; have pity then, my son, on the old Irrouba, and repair at least that part of the roof which is above my bed, it is all I ask, and the good Being will bless thee. And what was her bed? Alas! three boards grossly connected, and on which was disposed a bundle of parasite plant of the country, named *Barbe-Espagnole*. The roof of thy hut is almost uncovered, the sleet and the rain beat against thy miserable bed; thy master sees all this, and yet has no compassion for the poor Irrouba."

6. Of slavery in general, and particularly, &c. p. 180.

7. Voyage in Senegal, by Durand, 4to. Paris, 1802. p. 368.

8. See Robin, vol. II, p. 203.

9. Thoughts upon the African slave trade.

10. An abstract of the evidence, &c. p. 91, and following.

11. Ledyard, vol. II, p. 340.

12. History of Loango, by Proyart, 1766, 8vo. Paris. p. 59, and following; p. 73.

13. Fragments of a voyage in Africa, by Golberry, 2 vol, 8vo. Paris, 1802, vol. II, p. 391, and following.

14. In 4to. London, 1787.

15. Demanet, p. 11.

16. Long, vol. II, p. 416.

17. Voyage into the Interior of Africa, by Mungo Park, vol. II, p. 8 and 10.

18. Ibid. p. 11.

19. Stedman, vol. III, p. 66.

20. Night Cap, by Mercier, vol. II, article, *morals*.

21. Dickson's *Letters on Slavery,* 1789, p. 20, and following.

22. Stedman, vol. III, p. 70 and 76.

23. Cowry, p. 27.

24. Stedman, vol. I, p. 270.

25. Ibid. vol. I, p. 270.

26. Dickson, p. 180.

27. Description of the French portion of St. Domingo, by Moreau St. Mery, vol. I, p. 416, and following.

28. St. Mery, p. 44. A few pages before this, he praises their habits of cleanliness.

29. Hervey's Meditations, p. 151.

30. Voyage of discovery in the Interior of Africa, by Houghton and Mungo Park, p. 180.

31. Essay on the agriculture and commerce of the isles of France and Reunion, 8vo. Rouen, 1803, p. 37.

32. Among the other works we may consult an abstract of the evidence delivered before a select committee of the house of commons, in 1790 and 1791, 8vo. London, 1791, particularly p. 91, and following.

Chapter V

Talents of the negroes for arts and trades. Political societies organized among the Negroes.

Bosman, Bruo, Barbet, Holben, James Lyn, Kiernan, Dalrymple, Towne, Wadstrom, Falconbridge, Wilson, Clarkson, Durand, Stedman, Mungo Park, Ledyard, Lucas, Houghton, Horneman,[1] all of whom were acquainted with the blacks, and having lived among them in Africa, give testimony of their talents and industry. Moreau St. Mery thinks they are capable of succeeding in the mechanical and liberal arts.[2] Examine the authors we have cited: from the general History of voyages by Prevot, and the Universal History, the production of an English author, and the narrative of depositions made at the bar of Parliament; all speak, of the dexterity with which negroes tan and dye leather, prepare indigo and soap, make cordage, fine tissue, excellent pottery ware, although ignorant of the turning machine; arms of white metal, instruments of agriculture, and curious works in gold, silver and steel: they particularly excel in filigrane work.[3] One of the most striking proofs of their talents in this line, is their method of constructing an anchor for a vessel.[4] At Juida, they make combs of a single piece of ivory which are nearly two metres or six feet in length.[5]

Dickson, who knew among them jewellers and skilful watch-makers, speaks with admiration of a wooden lock executed by a negroe.[6]

In a learned dissertation on the floating bricks of the ancients, by Fabroni, I find this passage: "It is difficult to conceive in what manner the ancient inhabitants of Ireland and the Orcades, could construct

55

towers of earth and bake them on the same spot? This however is still practised by some negroes on the coast of Africa."[7]

Golberry, who is more particular than other travellers, in his details concerning African industry, says, that the stuffs made by them are very fine and of a rare beauty. The most ingenious are the Mandingoles and Bamboukains: their jars and mats are executed with much taste. With the same instruments they make the grossest works in iron, and the most elegant in gold: they thin leather in such a manner as to render it as flexible as paper; and the only instrument they employ, in the most delicate workmanship, is a very simple knife.[8]

The same observations apply to the negroes of Asia, of Malacca, and other parts of India. They send black and white slaves to Manilla. Sandoval, who was there, assures us, that all have a great aptitude for improvement, particularly in music. Their women excel in needlework.[9]

Lescalier, in travelling in the continent of Asia, found that the negroes with long hair, are well educated, because they have schools. Like the other Indians, they manufacture fine muslins, which are sent by this country to Europe. France, said another traveller, is full of stuffs made by negro slaves.[10]

In reading Winterbottom, Ledyard, Lucas, Houghton, Mungo Park and Horneman, we find that the inhabitants of the interior of Africa, are more virtuous and more civilized than those of the coasts; surpass them also in the preparations of wool, leather, wood and metals; in weaving, dying and sewing. Besides rural labors, which occupy them much, they have manufactories, and extract ore from minerals. The inhabitants of the country of Haissa, who, according to Horneman, are the most intelligent people of Africa, give cutting instruments a keener edge than European artists; their files are superior to those of France or of England.[11]

These details already anticipate what we must think, when to degrade the blacks, Jefferson tells us, that no nation of them was ever civilized. A problem not yet solved, though doubtless not insoluble, is the method of adjusting the intellectual faculties and talents, so as not to suffer that corruption to germinate, which attend fashionable amusements, I do not say inevitably, but always follow in their train.

Be that as it may, in confining ourselves to the acceptation which the word sociability presents, that is, a disposition to live with men in a relation to mutual services, to the idea of a polished state, which has a regular form of government and religion; the security of persons and property, which puts under the protection of laws, or of usages having the force of law, the exercise of agricultural, mechanical or commercial arts; who can deny to many black people the qualities of a civilized people? Is it they, of whom Leon the African speaks, who on the mountains, have something of the savage, but in the plains, have built towns, where they cultivate the sciences and arts. In a narrative, found in the collection of Prevot, they are described as more improved than among European nations.[12]

Bosman, who found the country of Agonna, well governed by a woman,[13] speaks with raptures of the appearance of that Juida, of the number of towns, of their customs and industry. More than a century afterwards, his recital has been confirmed by Pruneau de Pomme Gouje, who praises the courage and ability of the inhabitants of this country.[14] The particulars of their life present more ceremonies and civilities than are found in China. Superiority of rank, has there, as in all other places, its proud pretensions; but generally, individuals in similar situations, kneel and bless each other.[15] Without approving these minute ceremonies, we must nevertheless perceive the features of a nation rescued from barbarism.

Denian, a French consul, who resided thirteen years in Juida, has assured me, that the government of this country, in cunning diplomacy is a rival to those in Europe, who have improved this pernicious art. What proofs of this do we find in the life of the celebrated Gingha or Zingha, queen of Angola, who died in 1663, in her 82d year. To acuteness of mind, she united a ferocious intrepidity.

Like most great criminals of her rank, in her old age, she proposed to expiate her crimes by remorse, which alas! could not restore life to the unhappy individuals whom she had doomed to death.

According to an opinion generally received among us, a nation is not civilized unless it have historians and annals. We do not pretend to place the negroes on a level with those, who, to the discoveries of all ages, of which they are heirs, add their own; but can it be inferred from this, that the negroes are incapable of becoming partners in the storehouse of human knowledge? If, because they are not possessors, they are incapable of becoming such, the descendants of the ancient Germans, Helvetians, Batavians and Gauls, would be still barbarians; for there was a time when they had nothing so good as the knots *quipos* of Mexico, or the runic stick of the Scandinavians. What did they then possess? The vague and figurative traditions of ages, similar to those of all negro tribes; and nevertheless they had, like all the Celts, of which they formed a portion, a name, political confederations, a regular government, national assemblies, and more especially, freedom.

We agree with the historian of Jamaica, that the state of civilization in every country can point out only in some respects, the degree of civilization; for applying this standard to England, his country, we might ask him, whether an unrepealed law, which authorizes a husband to sell his wife, be a symptom of an improved civilization? The same question may be applied to these Neronian laws, which have reduced the Irish catholics to the rank of Helots. Notwithstanding these stains which disfigure the British constitution, we cannot deny that it is one of those which best combines the security of the state with individual liberty: under forms less complicated, the same thing exists among many black nations, whom Long supposes not to possess the faculty of combining ideas.[16]

In many parts of the coast of Africa, there are very small kingdoms, where the chief has no more authority than the father of a family.[17] In Gambia, Bonden, and in other small states, the government is monarchical, but authority is tempered by the chiefs of tribes, without whose advice they can neither make war nor peace.[18]

The industrious race of Accas, who occupy the fertile promontory of Cape Verd, have an organized republic; and although separated by dry sands, from the king of Damel, they are often engaged with him in war. When the king of Damel had a dispute with the government of Senegal, from whom he no longer received *toll,* and when he lately treated with the English recently established at Goree, he proposed that they should aid him in subjugating this people: and to stimulate them to this project, he alleged that the people of Acca were not like the other negroes, submissive to a chief, but free as the French then were. This trait of African diplomacy was communicated to me by Broussonnet.

Such then are the people who have seized the complicated idea of a constitution, a government, a treaty and alliance. If they have not a better knowledge of politics, it is because it was first necessary to have an existence.

In the empire of Bornon, says the traveller Lucas, the monarchy is elective, as also in the government of Kachmi. When the chief dies, they entrust to three elders or notables, the right of choosing his successor among the children of the deceased, without regard to primogeniture. He who is elected is conducted by three elders to the dead body of the deceased, whose eulogium, or condemnation is pronounced according to his merit; and his successor is reminded that he shall be happy or miserable, according to the good or evil he has done to the people. Similar customs prevail among neighbouring tribes.[19]

The following anecdote naturally presents itself. The commandant of a Portuguese fort, who expected the arrival of the envoy of an African king, orders the most sumptuous preparations, that he may be dazzled with the glare of opulence. The envoy arrives: he is introduced to a richly ornamented saloon. The commandant is seated under a canopy. The negro ambassador was not invited to sit down. He makes a sign, and instantly two of his slaves place their hands upon the floor, the back of which serves him as a seat. Thy king, said the commander to him, is he as powerful as our king of Portugal? My king, replies the negro, has a hundred servants like the king of Portugal, a thousand like thee, one like me—and he instantly departs.[20]

Civilization is no doubt almost nothing in several of the negro states, where they do not speak to a little king but through a trumpet, and when he has dined, a herald announces that then the other potentates of the world may dine in their turn. The king of Kakojs is no more than a barbarian, who uniting all power in his own person, judges all causes, swallows a cup of wine of the palm-tree at each sentence he pronounces, without which it would be illegal, and often terminates fifty processes at a single setting.[21] But the ancestors of civilized whites were also barbarians. Compare the situation of Russia in the fifteenth century to that of the present. It is now known that in the regions of Africa, there are states where the social arts have made progress. New proofs have given the highest degree of evidence to this fact.

The Foulahs, whose kingdom is about sixty myriameters in length, and thirty-nine in breadth, have towns with a considerable population. Temboo, the capital, has seven thousand inhabitants: Islamism, there speeding its errors, has introduced books chiefly on religion and jurisprudence. In Temboo, Laby, and almost all the towns of Foulahs, and in the empire of Banon, there are schools.[22] According to Mungo Park, the negroes love instruction: they have advocates to defend their slaves, who are brought before the tribunals:[23] domesticity is unknown among them, and slavery is mild. This traveller found magnificence in the bosom of Africa, at Sego, a town of thirty thousand souls, although, in every respect inferior to Jenne, to Tombuctoo and Houssa. It became necessary to pay no attention to narratives in other respects concordant, which we have till the present time obtained concerning these three towns.

With these African nations, we ought to associate the Boushouanas, visited by Barrow, who praises their character, the mildness of their manners, and the happiness they enjoy: they have stepped beyond those bounds which separate the savage from the civilized man, and their moral improvement is such, that, in this country, the zeal of christian missionaries might be usefully exercised. Litaken, their capital town, having from ten to fifteen thousand souls, is situated at 125 myriameters from the Cape. The government is patriarchal; the chief has a right to name his successor, but in all things he acts according to the will of the people, which is communicated to him by a council of old men; for amongst the Boushouanas, old age and authority, are, as among the ancients, words almost synonimous.[24] It was unfortunate that unpleasant circumstances, of which Barrow gives the detail, prevented him from visiting the Barrolons, who were described to him as more civilized in civilization, who have no idea of slavery, and among whom are found great towns where different arts flourish.[25] I forgot to mention what we find in the narrative of Golberry, that in Africa there are no beggars, except the blind, who sing airs, or recite passages of the Koran.[26]

The colonists reproach the negro Maroons, so improperly called rebels, whether of Surinam, or of the mountain of Jamaica, of not having organized a civilized society. The answer to this objection is anticipated by what we have read. Besides, can we suppose that the peaceable arts will be cultivated by a wandering people, always concealed in forests or in marshes; always occupied in seeking nourishment and defending themselves against their oppressors, who are true rebels. Yes, rebels against the sentiments of justice and of nature.

It will be objected, perhaps, that the people of Hayti have not been able to establish a permanent form of government, and that they tear each other with their own hands; but during the storm of our revolution, sacred in its principles, calumniated only by those whose efforts were directed to destroy its results; have we not witnessed every species of cruelty? Was not the nation, to use the expression of a deputy, put under regulated torture, and a volcano kindled to devour many generations? Besides, if a foreign hand has often brandished amongst us the torch of discord, how many such may have thus been employed at St. Domingo. Six thousand negroes or mulattoes, associated themselves formerly to the Caribs concentered in the isles of St. Vincent and Domingo. Those black Caribs are a robust people, and proud of their independence.[27] Every thing told of them by travellers, announces that their social state would rapidly improve, if they did not fear, and with reason, the rapacity of Europe, and if they could enjoy in peace the fruits of the field, which they would cultivate without trouble. During a century, they have constantly struggled against the elements and tyrants.

The province of Fernanbouc, in South America, has exhibited a body politic, formed by negroes, whom Malte-Brun still very improperly calls *rebels* and *revolters,* in a curious memoir on Brasil, according to the authority of Borlochus and Rochapitta, the one a Dutchman and the other a Portuguese, and which is inserted in the translation of Barrow's work.

Between the years 1620 and 1630, some fugitive negroes, united with some Brasilians, had formed two free states, the great and the little *Palmares,* thus named from the quantity of palm-trees they had there planted. In 1644, the great Palmares was almost entirely destroyed by the Hollanders. And a Portuguese historian, who appears, says Malte-Brun, not to have known the origin of these tribes, takes their restoration in 1650, for their real commencement.

At the close of the war with the Hollanders, the slaves of the neighbourhood of Fernanbouc, accustomed to sufferings and to combat, resolved to form an establishment which would guarantee their liberty. Forty of them laid the foundation, and their numbers soon increased by the addition of a multitude of other negroes and mulattoes; but having no women, they committed, over a vast extent of country, a rape similar to that of the Sabines. Having become formidable to all their neighbours, the Palmarisians adopted a form of worship, which, if we may so say, was a parody on christianity. They formed a constitution, laws, and tribunals, and elected a chief, named *Zombi,* which signifies powerful, whose authority, though elective, was for life. They fortified their villages, situated on eminences, and particularly their capital whose population consisted of 20,000 souls; they reared domestic animals, and much poultry. Barloeus describes their gardens, their cultivation of the sugarcane, their potatoes, manioc and millet, the reaping of which was signalized by *fetes* and songs of mirth.

Almost fifty years elapsed, and not sixty, as stated by the author of the memoir, before they were attacked. But in 1696, the Portuguese prepared an expedition against the Palmarisians. The latter having their Zombi or chief at their head, performed prodigies of valor. At last overcome by a superior force, some sought death that they might not survive the loss of their liberty; others, delivered up to the rage of conquerors, were sold and dispersed. Thus was extinguished a republic, which might have revolutionized the new world; a republic worthy of a better fate.

At the end of the 17th century, the colony of Palmares was destroyed by iniquity. At the close of the 18th century, benevolence and justice have created another at Sierra-Leone, of which we shall give some account.

From the year 1761, Franklin had established it as a principle, that the labour of a free man costs less and produces more, than that of a slave. Smith and Dupont de Nemours, have developed this idea by minute calculations; the one in his wealth of nations, the other in the sixth volume of the *Ephemerides* of a citizen, published in 1771. He therein first disclosed his project of substituting for the slave trade, civilization in the bosom of Africa, by forming upon the coasts, establishments of free negroes, for the cultivation of colonial productions.

This idea embraced by Fothergill, has been again illustrated by Demanet, Golberry, and by Postlewaight, who, in the two last editions of his commercial dictionary, has shewn himself successively the antagonist and apologist of negroes. By Pruneau de Pomme Gouje, who, having had the misfortune of being engaged in the slave trade, has asked pardon from God and from the human race. 3d. By Pelletan, who considers this colonization as the sure means of changing the face of desolated countries. 4th. By Wadstrom, who has published the result of a voyage which he made in Africa with Sparrman. But Dr. Isert, had already tried to execute it at Aquapin, on the banks of the Volta, and his letters present an affecting picture of the habits of those negro colonists. There have been successors to this establishment, but with its present situation I am totally unacquainted.

In 1792, the English proposed to form a free colony at Bulam. This attempt failed like that at Cayenne in 1763, and by the same causes; a bad plan, a wretched execution, and a want of foresight. Beaver, who published in detail, a relation of this establishment commenced at Bulam, proves the possibility and points out the means of success. This production furnishes an answer to Barre St. Venant, who questions this possibility, if already he had not been refuted by the existence of a colony at Sierra-Leone.

Neither Demanet nor Postlewaight, had designated the place fit for the execution of this project. Doctor Smeatham selected Sierra-Leone, situated between the 8th and 9th degree of north latitude, whose soil is fertile and climate temperate. A territory sufficiently large was obtained from two small neighbouring kings. Grandville Sharp formed a plan in union with the London society, of which Jonas Hanway was president, for the relief of *poor blacks*. Thus the principal co-operators are Smeatham, who, after a residence of four years in Africa, returned to Europe, to concert measures relative to his plan of free colonies. He does in 1786. He did not write, but his conduct was a model of practical virtue, and to him we are indebted for this maxim, which is better than some hundred books: "If every individual were convinced that he would find his own happiness in labouring for that of others, the human race would soon be blest."

Thornton had formed the project of transporting emancipated negroes from America to Africa.

5th. The same had been proposed by Afzelius, the botanist, and by Nordenskiold, the mineralogist, both Swedes; the last of whom died in Africa; the other is actually in Europe.

6th. By Grandville Sharp, who, in 1788, at his own expence, sent a vessel of 180 tons with succours to Sierra-Leone. He had previously published his plan of a constitution, and of legislation for the colonies.[28] To these respectable names we must join those of Wilberforce, Clarkson, and others, who have assisted with money, with writings, and with counsels, in the execution of this plan. These are they whose indefatigable zeal, and unwearied perseverance, obtained the bill for the abolition of the slave-trade.

The legislature will doubtless adopt measures for its execution, the necessity of which is demonstrated by Wilberforce, in a letter to his constituents in Yorkshire.[29] This abolition will for ever recall the most honourable trait of his public life. It would be worthy of him to turn his views towards that isle which has been martyred for so many ages;— towards Ireland, where three millions of individuals are politically disinherited, calumniated, and abused as catholics, by the government of a nation which has so much boasted of its liberty and its tolerance.

One of the constitutional articles of Sierra-Leone excludes Europeans, whose corrupting influence is generally dreaded, and none are admitted but the agents of the company. The first embarkation in 1786, was composed of some whites necessary for the direction of the establishment, and 400 negroes. This experiment met with very little success until it was aided by another, established on better principles, and which, in 1791, was incorporated by an act of parliament. The following year 1131 blacks, from Nova-Scotia were there transported, who, in the revolutionary war of America, had fought for England. Many of them were from Sierra-Leone; they gazed with keen emotions on their native soil, from which they had been dragged in their infancy, and as the rising colony was sometimes visited by the neighbouring tribes, an aged mother recognized her son, and, in tears, threw herself into his arms. The natives of this coast soon united themselves to those who were brought from Nova-Scotia. Some of the latter are good cannoneers, and what is far preferable, they shew activity and intelligence in agricultural and industrious occupations. The chief place *Free-Town,* ten years ago, had already new streets, and four hundred houses, with a garden to each. Not far distant is *Grandville-Town,* which bears the name of that estimable philanthropist Grandville-Sharp.

In the year 1794, they counted in their schools about 300 scholars, of whom 40 were natives, and almost all were endowed with a ready conception. They were taught reading, writing and arithmetic. The girls were besides instructed in those branches which belong to their sex, and the boys were taught geography and the elements of geometry.

Most of the negroes who came from America, being Methodists or Baptists, they have *meeting-houses,* where they worship; and the inspection of five or six preachers—blacks, has powerfully contributed to the support of good order.

The negroes exercise civil functions, and among others those of jurymen, with firmness, mildness, and justice—for trial by jury is established in this colony. They even shew themselves very jealous of their rights. The governor, by his own authority, having ordered some punishments to be inflicted, the condemned declared that they must be judged by a verdict of their peers. In general, they are pious, sober, correct, good husbands and good fathers. They give numberless proofs of their honest sentiments, and notwithstanding the disastrous events of the war[30] and of the elements which have ravaged this colony, they there enjoy all the advantages of a social state. These facts are extracted from reports, published yearly by the company at Sierra-

Leone,[31] of which a collection was presented to me by the celebrated Wilberforce. In October 1800, the colony increased by an addition of Maroons from Jamaica, which were deported there contrary to the faith of the treaty which they had made with general Walpole, and in opposition to their reclamations.

It appears, that all things otherwise equal, the countries where we find least energy and industry, are those where an excessive heat inclines to indolence; where physical wants, very confined by reason of this temperature, are sufficiently gratified in the abundance of consumeable commodities. It also appears that owing to these causes, slavery ought to be confined to burning climates, and that liberty, whether political, or civil, ought to meet with more obstacles between the tropics, than in higher latitudes: But who would not smile at the gravity with which Barre St. Venant assures us, "that the negroes, incapable of advancing a single step towards civilization, shall be after 20,000 centuries, that which they were 20,000 thousand centuries ago," the disgrace and misfortune of the human race? Accumulated facts refute this planter, so well informed what the negroes were before they had an existence, and who so prophetically reveals what they will be after the lapse of 20,000 centuries. Long since the natives of America would have arrived at a state of the most complete civilization, if there had been destined for this great purpose, a hundreth part, of the efforts, of the money and time, which have been employed in tearing the flesh, and butchering many millions of unfortunates, whose blood calls for vengeance against Europe.

Notes

1. Abstract of the evidence, &c. p. 89; Clarkson, p. 125; Stedman, ch. 26, Durand, p. 368, and following: History of Loango, by Bogart. p. 107; Mungo Park, vol. II, p. 35, 39, and 40.

2. Topographical description of St. Domingo, vol. I, p. 90.

3. Prevot, vol. I, p. 3, 4, 5; and Universal History, 4to. edit. vol. 17, ch. 71; Beaver, p. 327.

4. Prevot, vol. II, p. 421.

5. Description de la Negritie, par *P.D.P.* Pruneau de Pomme Gouje, 8vo. Paris, 1789.

6. Dickson, p. 74.

7. Le Magaz, Encycloped. vol. II, 1 Brum. an. 7. p. 335.

8. Fragments of a voyage in Africa, by Golberry, 2 vol. 8vo. Paris, 1802, vol. I, p. 413, and following; vol. II, p. 380, &c.

9. Sandoval, part I, vol. II, c. xx, p. 205.

10. Journal d'un voyage aux Indes, sur l'escadre de du Quesne, vol. II, p. 214.

11. Mungo Park, vol. II, p. 35, 39, 40. The Journal of Frederic Horneman's Travels, 4to. London, 1802, p. 38, and following.

12. Prevot, vol. IV, p. 283.

13. Bosman, 4 vols. p. 283.

14. Description de la Nigritie, par D.P. 8vo. Paris, 1789.

15. Bosman, lettre 18.

16. Long, vol. II, p. 377, and 378.

17. Beaver, p. 328.

18. Mungo Park, p. 128.

19. Lucas, vol. I, p. 190.

20. Anecdote related by Bernardin St. Pierre. The author of *African Anecdotes* relates the same thing of Zingha. He adds, that when she arose, the slave remained in the same posture. Being reminded of this, she replied, the sister of a king never sits twice on the same seat.

21. History of Loango, &c.

22. Lucas and Ledyard, vol. I, p. 190, and following. Substance of the report, p. 136.

23. Mungo Park, p. 13. and 37.

24. Voyage a la Cochinchine, vol. I, p. 289, and following.

25. Ibid. p. 319, and following.

26. Fragment d'un voyage fait en Afrique, 2 vols. 8vo. Paris, 1802, vols. II, p. 400.

27. De l'influence de la decouverte de l'Amerique sur le bonheur du genre humain, par Le Gentil, 8vo. Paris, 1788, p. 74, and following.

28. A short sketch of temporary regulations for the intended settlement on the coast of Africa, &c.

29. A letter on the abolition of the slave-trade, addressed to the freeholders and other inhabitants of Yorkshire, by W. Wilberforce, 8vo. London, 1807.

30. In 1794, a French squadron occupied in destroying the English establishments on the western coast of Africa, partly destroyed this colony at Sierra-Leone. This fact was the subject of grave inculpation. In January 1806, I read a memoir at the Institute, in which from an examination of the registers of the commandant of the squadron, I proved that his attack against Sierra-Leone was the result of error. He believed that it was a mercantile enterprize, and not a philanthropic establishment. This memoir was published in the *Decade Philosophique,* No. 67, and afterwards printed separately.

31. Substance of the report delivered by the court of direction of the Sierra-Leone company, and particularly that of 1794, p. 55, and following.

Chapter VI

Literature of Negroes.

Wilberforce, in conjunction with many members of the society occupied with the education of Africans, has established for them a kind of college at Clapham, which is about four leagues distant from London. The first placed there were twenty-one young negroes, sent by the governor of Sierra Leone. I visited this establishment in 1802, to examine the progress of the scholars, and I found that between them and European children there existed no difference but that of colour. The same observation has been made, 1st, at Paris, in the ancient college of La Marche, where Coesnon, formerly professor of the university, had united a certain number of negro children. Many members of the National Institute, who have also carefully examined this college, and traced the progress of the scholars in all the circumstances of life, in their particular classes, and public exercises, will give testimony to the truth of my assertion.

2nd. This was proven at a school in Philadelphia, by Brissot,[1] a man calumniated with fury, and then judicially assassinated—a true republican, of rigid probity, who died as he had lived—poor.

3rd. The same fact has been established at Boston, by Giraud, the French consul there, in a school of 400 negro children, who are educated separately from whites. The law authorizes their assembling with the young white children, but owing to a hereditary prejudice not yet totally effaced, they torment the blacks. Sound reason proves, that this conduct is disgraceful to the whites only, and particularly so to the

Free Masons in this town, who fraternize among themselves, but who have never once visited an African lodge. This lodge shared equal honours when at the funeral ceremony for Washington, it formed a part of the cavalcade.

Among the number of authors, who believe that the intellectual faculties of negroes are susceptible of the same developement as those of whites. I forgot to cite Ramsay,[2] Hawker,[3] and Beckford.[4] The honest Wadstrom pretended, that in this respect, the blacks have a superiority;[5] and Skipwith, the American consul, is of the same opinion.

Clenard counted at Lisbon, more Moors and negroes than whites; and these blacks, said he, are worse than brutes.[6] Things are wonderfully changed. Correa de Serra, the learned secretary of the Academy at Portugal, informs us that several negroes, have been learned lawyers, preachers, and professors; and at Lisbon, Rio-Janeiro, and in other Portuguese possessions, have been signalized by their talents. In 1717, the negro Don Juan Latino, taught the Latin language at Seville. He lived to the age of 117.[7] The brutality of the Africans, of which Clenard speaks, was then only the result of misery and oppression— besides, he himself acknowledges their capacity for improvement. "I instruct, says he, my negro slaves in literature, and in manumitting them; I shall have at some future day, like Crassus, my *Diphilus,* and like Cicero, my *Tyro;* they already write very well, and begin to understand Latin: the ablest reads to me at table.[8]

Lobo, Durand, Demanet, who resided a long time, the first in Abyssina, the others in Guinea, found negroes with a keen and penetrating mind, a sound judgment, taste, and delicacy.[9] Different writers have collected brilliant repartees and answers truly philosophical made by blacks.—Such is the following, cited by Bryan Edwards: —a slave was suddenly awaked by his master, who said, *Dost thou not hear thy master who calls thee?* The poor negro opens his eyes, and immediately shuts them, saying, *Sleep has no master.*

With respect to their intelligence in business, it is well known in the Levant. Michaud, the elder, told me that he had seen them in different parts of the Persian gulph, as heads of great commercial houses, receiving orders, expediting vessels to all the different parts of the Indian coast. Michaud had purchased at Philadelphia, and brought into France, a young negro from the interior of Africa, at an age when his memory had already acquired some geographical ideas of the country where he was born. This naturalist paid great attention to his education, and proposed, when it was finished, to send him back to his native country, as a traveller to explain regions little known; but Michaud died on the coast of Madagascar, and this negro, who accompanied him, was inhumanly sold. I know not whether the reclamations which the younger Michaud made against this barbarous action has been favoured.

Among the Turks, the negroes sometimes arrive at the most eminent offices. Different writers have given the same account of Kislar-Aga, who, in 1730, was chief of the black eunuchs of the Porte, and have described him as possessing great wisdom and profound knowledge.[10]

Adanson, astonished to hear the negroes of Senegal mention a great number of stars, and reason pertinently concerning them, believes that if they had good instruments, they would become good astronomers.[11]

On different parts of the coast there are negroes who speak two or three languages, and are interpreters.[12] In general they have a very retentive memory. This has been remarked by Villaut, and by other travellers.[13] Stedman knew a negro, who could repeat from memory the Alcoran. The same thing is told of Job Ben Solomon, son of the Mahometan king of Bunda, on the Gambia. Solomon taken in 1730, was brought to America, and sold in Maryland. A train of extraordinary adventures, which may be read in the *More lak,* brought him to England, where his dignified air, amenity of character and talents, gained him friends, and among others, Hans Sloane, baronet, for whom he translated several Arabic manuscripts. After being received with distinction at the court of St. James, the African company, interested in his fate, in 1734, reconducted him to Bunda. One of the uncles of Solomon embracing him, said, during sixty years thou art the first slave that I have seen return from the American isles. He wrote letters to all his friends in Europe, and in the new world, which were translated and perused with interest. At his father's death he became his successor, and was beloved in his states.[14]

The son of the king Nimbana, who came to England to study, had learnt different sciences with rapid success, and in a very short time was so well acquainted with Hebrew as to be able to read the bible in the original. This young man, who gave such promising hopes, died a short time after his return to Africa.

Ramsay, who passed twenty years in the midst of negroes, says, they possess the mimic art to such a degree, that they can rival our modern Garricks. Labat assures us that they are naturally eloquent.

Poivre was often astonished with specimens of this talent in the Madeasses, and Rochon has thought proper to insert in his voyage to Madagascar, the discourse of one of their chiefs, which even after that of Logan, may be read with pleasure.[15]

Stedman, who thinks them capable of great improvement, and who praises more particularly their poetical and musical talents, enumerates their wind and stringed instruments, which amounts to eighteen in number;[16] and, nevertheless, we do not find in the list, the famous *balafou,*[17] formed of twenty pipes of hard wood, which gradually diminish, and emit a sound similar to that of a small organ.

Grainger describes a kind of guitar invented by the negroes, on which they play airs, which inspire a sweet and sentimental melancholy,[18] the music of afflicted hearts. The passion of negroes for the song, does not prove that they are happy. This is observed by Benjamin Rush, in his description of the maladies resulting from their state of sorrow and misfortune.[19]

Dr. Gall has assured me, that in negroes the organs of music and mathematics are wanting. When, on the first head, I observed that one of the most distinguishing characters of the negroes, is their invincible taste for music, he acknowledged the fact, but denied that they have capacity for improving this fine art. But is not the energy of this inclination an incontestable proof of talent? It is by experience that men succeed in studies to which they were allured by a strong bias, a decided propensity. Who can say how far the negroes may excel in this art, when the knowledge of Europe comes within their reach? Perhaps they will yet have their Glucks and Piccinis. Already Gosses has not disdained to insert, in his *Camp de Grand Pre,* an air of the negroes of St. Domingo.

France had formerly her *Trouveres* and *Troubadours,* as Germany, her *Min Singer,* and Scotland her *Minstrels.* Negroes have theirs, named *Griots,* who attend kings, and like the others, praise and lie with wit. Their women, named *Griotes,* perform almost the same trade as the *Almees* in Egypt, and the Bagaders in India. This forms another trait of resemblance between them and the travelling women of the Troubadours. But these *Trouveres, Min-Singers,* and *Minstrels,* were the forerunners of Malherbe, Corneille, Racine, Shakespeare, Pope, Gesner, Klopstock, Wieland, &c. In all countries, genius is a spark concealed in the bosom of a flint, which bursts forth at the stroke of the steel.

In the 16th century, appeared Louisa Labbé de Lyon, surnamed the fine *rope maker,* in allusion to the employment of her husband.

In the 17th century, Billan, surnamed master Adam, a joiner at Never; and Hubert Pott, a simple workman in Holland.

Beronicius, a chimney-sweeper in the same country, exhibited the phenomenon of a poetic genius, united to a profession which generally rejects the idea of a cultivated mind; the nicest taste must give them a place in Parnassus, though it cannot assign them the first. The traveller Pratt, proclaims Hubert Pott, the father of elegiac poetry, in Holland;[20] and in the Middlebury edition of the works of Beronicius, the print which serves as a frontispiece, represents Apollo crowning the poet chimney-sweeper with laurels.[21]

A servant of Glats, in Silesia, has lately excited the public attention by his romances.[22] Bloomfield, a ploughman, has published a volume of poetry which has undergone several editions, and a part of which has been translated into our language.[23] Greensted, a female servant at Maidstone, and Anne Yearsley, a simple milkmaid of Bristol, are already placed in the rank of poets. The misfortunes of negroes form the subject of the muse of the last mentioned author, whose works have gone through four editions. We have also witnessed some of those Africans, whom iniquity destines to contempt and misfortune, overcome the obstacles connected with their situation, and exhibit a great expansion of mind. Several have entered the list of authors.

In 1787, when Toderini published three volumes on the literature of the Turks,[24] many individuals who doubted whether there was one learned person among them, were surprised to find that Constantinople possesses thirteen public libraries. Will the surprise be less in France, when works are announced to be composed by negroes and mulattoes? Among the latter, I could name Castaing, who has exhibited poetic genius. His pieces ornament different editions of poetry. Barbaud-Royer, Boisrond, the author of the *Precis des Gemissements des Sangmeles;*[25] who announces himself as belonging to this class; and Michel Mina, a mulatto of St. Domingo. Julien Raymond, likewise a mulatto, was also associated with the class of moral and political sciences, for the section of legislation. Without being able to justify in every respect the conduct of Raymond, we may praise the energy with which he defended men of colour and free negroes. He has published many works, of which the greatest part relates to the History of St. Domingo, which may serve as an antidote to the impostures circulated by the colonists.[26]

I ought not to forget the negress Belinda, born in the charming country of Africa, from which she was torn at twelve years of age, and sold in America. Although, says she, I have been servant to a colonel for forty years, my labours have not procured me any comfort: I have not yet enjoyed the benefits of creation. With my poor daughter, I shall pass the remainder of my days in slavery and misery. For her and for myself I at last beg freedom. Such is the substance of the petition, which, in 1782, she addressed to the legislature of Massachusetts. The authors of the American Museum, have preserved this petition, written without art, but dictated by the eloquence of grief, and therefore more fit to move the heart to pity. I could also make mention of the negro Cesar, of North Carolina, author of different pieces of printed poetry, which have become popular, like those of Bloomfield.

The number of negro writers is greater than that of mulattoes, and, in general they have shewn more zeal to avenge their African compatriots. We shall see proofs of this in the attieles *Othello,* Sancho, Vassa, Cugoana, Phillis Wheatley. Blumenbach obligingly communicated to me the works of two or three negroes, which I could not procure. My researches have made me acquainted with other negroes, some of whom have written nothing, but whose superiority of talents and extent of knowledge, entitle them to a place in history. In this number we find only one or two mulattoes, and a negro with long hair. Marcel, the director of the imperial printing press, who published at Cairo, an edition of Logman's Fables,[27] believes that this slave was an Abyssinian or Ethiopian, and consequently, says he, one of those black slaves, with thick lips and frizzled hair, from the interior of Africa, who, being sold to the Hebrews, was a keeper of flocks in Palestine. The editor presumes that Esop, Αισοποσ, which is nothing more than a corruption of the word Αιθιοψ, Αιθιτοποσ, Ethiopian, might be Logman himself.[28] We do not well perceive with what proof this assertion is corroborated; of the Fables attributed to him, the 17th and 23d relate to negroes; but was the author a negro? This is doubtful.

In adopting this hypothesis, I might have swelled my list with the names of all the Ethiopians recorded in history. The works of Ludolf and Lacroze, prevent me from entering into a detail on this subject.[29] I have thought proper to make mention of the negroes of modern times, since the commencement of colonial slavery, and there is one concerning whom I have only presumptive evidence, and nothing certain.

Notes

1. His travels, vol. II, p. 2.
2. Objections to the abolition of the slave trade, with answers, by Ramsay, 8vo. London, 1778, vol. II.
3. Sermon, 4to. in 1789.
4. Remarks upon the situation of the negroes in Jamaica, 8vo. London, 1788, p. 34, and following.
5. Observations on the slave trade, 8vo. London, 1789.
6. Varietés litteraries, 8vo. Paris, vol. I, p. 39, and 88.
7. Fact communicated by Mr. Lasteyrie.
8. Ibid. p. 88.
9. Durand, p. 58. Demanet, Histoire de l'Afrique francaise, 2 vol. p. 3. Relation historique de l'Abyssinic par Lobo, 4to. Paris, 1728, p. 680.
10. Observations sur la religion, les loix, les mœurs, des Turcs, traduit de L'Anglais, par M. B. Londres, 1769, p. 98.
11. Voyage au Senegal, p. 149.
12. Clarkson, p. 125.
13. Prevot, vol. IV, p. 198.
14. Le More-lack, par le Cointe-Marsillac, 8vo. Paris, 1789, c. xv.
15. Voyage a Madagascar et aux Indes occidentales, par Rochon, 8vo. Paris, 3 vols. vol. I, p. 173, &c.
16. Stedman, c. xxvi.
17. Others write *balafeu* or *balafo,* and its companion is the spinnet.
18. The Sugar-Cane, a poem in four books, by James Grainger, 4to. 1764.
19. American Museum, vol. IV, p. 82.
20. Pratt, vol. II, p. 208.
21. Beronicius has made Latin poems; and his poem in two books, entitled Georgar, or the battle between the peasants and the great, has been translated in Holland verse, and reprinted in 8vo. at Middlebury, in 1766.
22. La Prusse litteraire, par Denina, article Peyneman.
23. Tales and Rural Songs, by Robert Bloomfield, translated by de la Vaisse, 8vo. Paris, 1802.
24. Literatura turchesca, d'all' abate Giambatista.
25. Par P. M. C. Sang-mele, 8vo.
26. Especially a work entitled, Origine des troubles de St. Domingo, par Raymond.
27. Fables de Logman, 8vo. au Cairo, 1799.
28. La Notice de l'editeur, p. 10 and 11.
29. Jobi Ludolfi, Historia Ethiopica, in fol. 1681. Francofurti ad Mœnum. Histoire du christianisme de Ethiop. par adeyssiere la Croze, 8vo. 1739. La Haye.

Chapter VII

Of Negroes and Mulattoes distinguished by their talents and their works.

Sonnerat affirms that the Indian painters are neither acquainted with perspective, nor with *clair-obscure,* although, they give a perfect finish to their works. Nevertheless Higiemonde, or Higiemondo, commonly named the *negro,* was known as an able artist, although, his compositions discovered less of art, than of nature. Such is the opinion given by Joachim de Sandrart, in his work entitled *Academia nobillissimæ artis pictoriæ.*[1] He calls them very celebrated *clarissimus.* Without mentioning the epoch at which he lived, the epithet *nigrum,* in the Latin edition of Sandrart, would be insufficient to prove that Higiemonde was a *negro.* How many whites in Europe, have the name of *black.* Our doubts are removed by an inspection of the figure of Higiemonde, engraved by Kilian, and inserted in the two works of Sandrart.[2] viz. The one we have cited; and his German treatise, in *three volumes, folio,* with the Italian title, *d'Academia Tedesca delle Architectura, Scultura Pillura,* &c.[3] But in the text of this last work I find nothing concerning Higiemonde. It appears that talents do not belong exclusively to any country, or to any particular race of men. We have seen at Paris, a Calmuck, named Fedre, who is the first painter of the court of Baden.

At Rome, the art of painting was interdicted to slaves. This is the reason why Pliny the Elder says, that he is not acquainted with a single individual who is distinguished in this branch, or in *torentique.*

Hannibal

The Czar Peter the first, during his travels, had an opportunity of knowing Annibal, the African negro, who had received a good education; and who, under this monarch, became in Russia, lieutenant general and director of artillery. He was decorated with the red ribband of the order of St. Alexander Nenski. Bernardin St. Pierre and colonel La Harpe, knew his son, a mulatto, who had the reputation of talents. In 1784, he was lieutenant general in a corps of artillery. It was he, who under the orders of prince Potemkin, minister at war, commenced the establishment of a port and fortress at Cherson, near the mouth of the Dnieper.

Amo

Antony William Amo, born in Guinea, was brought to Europe when very young, and the princess of Brunswick, Wolfenbuttle, took charge of his education. He embraced the Lutheran religion, pursued his studies at Halle, in Saxony, and at Wittemberg, and so distinguished himself by his good conduct and talents, that the rector and council of the university of the last mentioned town, thought themselves obliged to give a public testimony of these in a letter of felicitation. In this they remark, that Terence also was an African;—that many martyrs, doctors, and fathers of the church were born in the same country, where learning once flourished, and which, by losing the christian faith, again fell back into barbarism.

Amo, skilled in the knowledge of the Greek and Latin languages, delivered with success, private lectures on philosophy, which are highly praised in the same letter. In a syllabus, published by the Dean of the Philosophical Faculty, it is said of this learned negro, that having examined the system of ancients and moderns, he selected and taught all that was best of them.[4]

Amo became a doctor. In 1744, he supported a Thesis at Wittemberg, and published a dissertation on the absence of sensation in the soul, and their presence in the human body.[5] In a letter which the President addressed to him, he is named *vir nobillisme et clarissime.* This may be intended as a compliment, but it proves, at least, as well as the preceding, that the university of Wittemberg, concerning the difference of colour in the human species, did not possess those absurd prejudices of so many others who think themselves enlightened. He declares that the dissertation of Amo underwent no change, because it was well executed. The work indicates a mind exercised in reflection. The author endeavours to ascertain the difference of phænomena which take place in beings simply existing, and those endowed with life—a stone exists, but it is without life. It appears that our author had a particular predilection for abstruce discussions; for being appointed professor, he, the same year, supported a Thesis, analogous to the preceding, on the distinction which ought to be made between the operations of mind and those of sense.[6] The titles of these two dissertations prove, that Amo, the author of the first, was also the author of the second.

I have sought in vain to know what became of this negro, and what other works he published.

The ancient inhabitants of the Phillipines were blacks, if we are to believe the accounts given of these isles, and particularly that of Gemelli Cairer. If it be true, that he only travelled in his chamber, as some pretend to believe, his work is composed of good materials, and is acknowledged as correct. Many blacks with frizzled hair, enamoured of freedom, still inhabit the mountains and forests of those isles They have even given their name to the isle of *Negroes,* one of those which compose this cluster. Although the population is made up of Chinese, Europeans, Indians and Malays, the general colour is black, and when it is not sufficiently deep, the women, who in all countries call upon art to assist nature, and who arrive at the same end by different means, heighten the colour by the use of different drugs.[7]

Among the varieties produced by the mixture of different races, the *Tagals* are particularly distinguished, who resemble the Malays in stature, colour, and language. If this observation applies to Bagay, of whom we shall give some account, it may be doubted whether he was black. I must acknowledge my own uncertainty on this subject. Carreri places the Tagal language at the head of six, which are in greatest use in these isles. He cites a Tagal dictionary made by a Cordelier.[8] There is a vocabulary of this tongue printed in the work of Father Navarette. A third was published at Vienna, in 1803.[9]

In general the Philippines are too little known. It appears that the Spanish government had proposed to conceal from Europe, this portion of the globe, where it supports colleges and printing-offices, a regular administration and a numerous clergy. We have a very curious and much esteemed map of this country, of large dimensions, by Father Murello Velarde, a Jesuit, engraved at Manilla, by Nicholas de la Cruz Bagay, an Indian Tagal. It is this Bagay whom I propose to introduce into the representation. In an account annexed to this map, we find that the natives of this country have a great capacity for painting, sculpture, embroidery, and all the arts of design. The productions of Bagay may be presented as a proof of this assertion. This map has been published in a reduced size, by Lowitz, professor of mathematics, at Nuremberg. I would be ungrateful if I terminated this article without thanking Barbier du Bocage, who very obligingly communicated to me these maps, and a dictionary of the Tagal language.

L'Islet Geoffroy

L'Islet Geoffroy, a mulatto, is an officer of artillery, and guardian of the *Depot* of maps and plans of the Isle of France. The twenty-third of August, 1785, he was named correspondent of the academy of sciences. He is acknowledged as such in the *Connoissance des temps* for the year 1791, published in 1789, by this learned society, to whom Lislet regularly transmitted meteorological observations and sometimes hydrographical journals. The class of physical and mathematical science of the national institute, thought it their duty to adopt the members of the academy of sciences as correspondents and associates. By what fatality is it that Lislet forms the sole exception? It is owing to his colour? Let us banish a suspicion which would be an outrage against my colleagues. Certainly Lislet, during the last twenty years instead of losing reputation, has acquired new claims on the esteem of the learned.

His map of the Isles of France and Reunion, delineated according to astronomical observations, the geometrical operations of La Caille, and particular plans was published in 1797, year 5, by order of the minister of marine. A new edition corrected from drawings transmitted by the author, was published in 1802, year 10, it is the best map of those isles that has yet appeared.

In the almanac of the Isle of France, which I have not been able to find at Paris, Lislet has inserted several memoirs, and among others the description of Pitrebot, one of the highest mountains of the isle. This fact was communicated to me by Mr. Aubert du Petit Thouars, who resided ten years in this colony.

The Institute, which has become the Legatee, of several academies at Paris, will doubtless publish a precious collection of manuscript memoirs, deposited in the Archives. We find there the relation of a voyage of Lislet to the Bay of St. Luce, an island of Madagascar, it is accompanied with a map of this Bay, and of the Coast. He points out the exchangeable commodities, the resources which it presents, and which would increase, says he, if instead of exciting the natives to war, in order to have slaves, they would encourage industry by the hope of an advantageous commerce. The description he gives of the customs and manners of the Malgaches are very curious. They discover a man versed in botany, natural philosophy, geology and astronomy:—and yet this man never visited the continent to improve his taste and acquire knowledge. He has struggled against the obstacles created by the prejudices of the country. It is reasonable to suppose that he would have performed more if brought, in his youth, to Europe, and breathing the atmosphere of the learned, he had found around him something which would have powerfully stimulated his curiosity and fructified his genius.

Some person belonging to the expedition of Captain Baudin, informed me, that Lislet, having established a scientific society at the Isle of France, some whites refused to be members, merely because its founder was a black. Have they not proven by their conduct that they were unworthy of this honor?

James Derham

James Derham, originally a slave at Philadelphia, was transferred by his master, to a physician, who gave him a subaltern employment, as a preparer of drugs. During the American war, he was sold by this physician to a surgeon, and by the surgeon to doctor Robert Dove, of New Orleans. Derham, who had never been baptized, had this ceremony performed, and was received into the English church. Learned in languages, he speaks with facility, English, French and Spanish. In 1788, at the age of twenty-one years, he became the most distinguished physician at New-Orleans. "I conversed with him on medicine," says Dr. Rush, "and found him very learned. I thought I could give him information concerning the treatment of diseases, but I learned more from him than he could expect from me." The Pennsylvania society, established in favour of the blacks, thought it their duty, in 1789, to publish these facts, which are also related by Dickson.[10] In the domestic medicine of Buchan,[11] and in a work, named, *Medecine du voyageur*,[12] by Duplaint, we find an account of the cure for the bite of a rattle snake. I know not whether Derham was the discoverer, but it is a well-known fact, that for this we are indebted to a negro, who received his freedom from the general assembly of Carolina, who also decreed him an annuity of 100*l*. sterling.

Thomas Fuller

Thomas Fuller, born in Africa, and residing at the distance of four miles from Alexandria, in Virginia, not knowing how to read or write, excited surprise by the facility with which he performed the most difficult calculations. Of the different methods employed to put his talents to the proof, we select the following: One day he was asked, how many seconds of time have elapsed since the birth of an individual, who had lived seventy years, seven months and as many days? In a minute and a half he answered the question. One of the interrogators takes his pen, and after a long calculation, pretended that Fuller is deceived—that the number he mentioned was too great. No, replied the negro, the error is on your side, for you have forgotten the leap years. His answer is found to be correct. We are indebted for this information to Dr. Rush, a man equally respected in Europe and America. His letter is found in the voyage of Stedman,[13] and in the fifth volume of the *American Museum*,[14] which appeared several years ago. Thomas Fuller was then seventy years old. Brissot, who had known him in Virginia, gives the same testimony of his talents.[15] There are examples of other negroes, who, by memory performed the most difficult calculations, and for the execution of which the Europeans were obliged to have recourse to the rules of arithmetic.[16]

Othello

In 1788, Othello published at Baltimore, *an essay against the slavery of negroes.* "The European powers, (said he,) ought to unite in bolishing the infernal commerce of slaves: it is they who have covered Africa with desolation. They declaim against the people of Algiers, and they vilify, as barbarians, those who inhabit a corner of that portion of the globe, where ferocious Europeans go to buy and carry away men, for the purpose of torture; and these are the people who pretend they are christians, while they degrade themselves by acting the part of an executioner. Is not your conduct, adds Othello, when compared with your principles, a sacrilegious irony? When you dare to talk of civilization and the gospel, you pronounce your anathema. In you the superiority of power produces nothing but a superiority of brutality and barbarism. Weakness, which calls for protection, appears to provoke your inhumanity. Your fine political systems are sullied by the outrages committed against human nature and the divine majesty.

When America opposed the pretensions of England, she declared that all men have the same rights. After having manifested her hatred against tyrants, ought she to have abandoned her principles? We ought to bless the measures taken in Pennsylvania in favour of the negroes, and we must execrate those of South Carolina, who have lately prevented the slaves from learning to read. To whom shall these unfortunates then address themselves? The law either neglects or chastises them.

Othello paints in strong colours the grief and sighs of children, fathers, brothers, and husbands, dragged from the country which gave them birth—a country always dear to their heart, by the remembrance of a family and local impressions. So dear to them is it, that one of the articles of their superstitious credulity, is to imagine, that after death they will there return. With the happiness which they enjoyed in their native soil, Othello contrasts their horrible state in America; where, naked, hungry, and without instruction, they see all the evils of life accumulate on their heads. He hopes that their cries may reach to heaven, and that heaven may be propitious to their prayers. Few works can be compared to this of Othello's, for force of reasoning, and fire of eloquence; but what can reason and eloquence perform, when opposed by avarice and crimes?

Bannaker

Benjamin Bannaker, a negro of Maryland, established in Philadelphia, without any other encouragement than his passion for acquiring knowledge, without books, except the works of Ferguson, and the tables of Tobias Mayer, applied himself to astronomy. He published almanacs for the years 1794, and 1795, in 8vo. at Philadelphia, in which are calculated and exhibited the different aspects of the planets, a table of the motions of the sun and moon, their risings and settings, and the courses of the bodies of the planetary system. Bannaker has received his freedom. Imlay says, that in New England, he knew a negro skilled in astronomy, who had composed ephemerides. He does not mention his name. If it be Bannaker, it is another testimony of his talents. If it be some other, it is another evidence in favour of negroes.

Cugoano

Ottobah Cugoano, born on the coast of Fantin, in the town of Agimaque, relates that he was dragged from his country, with twenty other children of both sexes, by European robbers, who brandishing their pistols and sabres, threatened to kill them if they attempted to escape. They confined them with others, and soon, says he, I heard nothing but the clanging of chains, the sound of the whip, and the howlings of my fellow-prisoners. He was a slave at Grenada, and was indebted for his liberty, to the generosity of Lord Hoth, who carried him to England. He was there in 1788, in the service of Cosway, the first painter of the Prince of Wales. Piatoli, author of a treatise in Italian, on the *situation* and *dangers* of burial grounds, which Vicq D'Azir, at the request of Dalembert, translated into French. Piatoli, who, during a long residence at London, was particularly acquainted with Cugoano, then about forty years of age, and whose wife was an Englishwoman, praises highly this African; and speaks in strong terms of his piety, his mild character and modesty, his integrity and talents.

A long time a slave at Cugoano, he had shared the fate of those unfortunates, who are corrupted, and calumniated by the iniquity of the whites.

Like Othello, he paints the heart-rending spectacle of those unfortunate Africans, who are forced to bid an eternal adieu to their native soil—to fathers, mothers, husbands, brothers and children; invoking heaven and earth, throwing themselves, bathed in tears, into each others arms, giving the last embrace, and instantly torn from all that the heart holds dear. This spectacle, says he, would move the heart of monsters, but not of colonists.

At Grenada, he had seen negroes lacerated by the whip, because, instead of working at manual labour on Sunday, they had been at church. He had seen others whose teeth had been broken because they had sucked sugar cane. Of many particulars contained in the registers of the courts of justice, he cites the following: when the Guinea captains wanted provisions, or when the cargo was too great, their custom was to throw overboard those negroes who were sick, or those whose sale would bring least profit.

In 1780, a negro trader, detained by contrary winds on the American coast, and in distress, selected one hundred and thirty-two of his sick slaves, and threw them into the sea, tied together in pairs, that they might not escape by swimming. He hoped that the insurance company would indemnify him for his loss; and in the process to which this crime gave birth, he observed, that "the negroes cannot be considered in any other light than as beasts of burden, and to lighten a vessel it is permitted to throw overboard the least valuable effects."

Some of these unhappy wretches escaped from the hands of those who tied them, and precipitated themselves into the waves. One was saved by means of a cord, the extremity of which was thrown to him by the sailors of another vessel. The barbarous assassin of those innocents, had the audacity to claim him as his property; but, whether owing to justice, or to a sense of shame, the judges rejected his demand.[17]

Most authors, who had censured this commerce, had employed the only arms which belong to reason. A voice was raised to spread abroad the spirit of revealed religion, and to prove by the bible, that the stealing, sale and purchase of men, and their detention in a state of slavery, are crimes worthy of death; and this voice was that of Cugoano, who published his reflections in English, on the *slave-trade,* and the *slavery of negroes,* of which there is a French translation.

His work is not very methodical. There are repetitions, because grief is verbose. An individual deeply affected, is always afraid of not having said enough—of not being sufficiently understood. We see talents without cultivation, and to which a good education would have given great progress.

After some observations on the cause of the difference of colour and complexion in the human species, such as climate, soil and dietetic regimen, he asks, whether is it "more criminal to be black or white, than to wear a black or a white coat. Whether colour and bodily form give a right to enslave men, whose vices are the work of colonists, for in a state of freedom, and profiting by the advantages of a christian education, they would be conducted to all that is good, useful and just; but as the colonists do not see, except through the veil of avarice and cupidity, every slave has the imperscriptible right of rescuing himself from their tyranny."

"The negroes have never crossed the seas to steal white men; if their conduct had been like that of other European nations, the cry of robbers and assassins, would from all quarters have been raised against them. They complain of barbarism, whilst their conduct towards negroes is horribly barbarous. Those odious epithets belong to them. The European factories in Africa, says Cugoano, are nothing but caverns of thieves and murderers. To steal men, to rob them of their liberty, is worse than to plunder them of their goods. In this Europe, which is called civilized, they chain or hang thieves, and send assassins to the scaffold; and if the negro traders and colonists be exempt from trial, it is because the people and governors are their accomplices, for the laws encourage the slave-trade and tolerate slavery. On national crimes heaven sometimes inflicts national punishments. Besides, injustice is sooner or later fatal to its authors. This idea which is conformable to the great plan of religion, is well developed by our author. He predicts that the wrath of heaven will particularly be directed against England, which, in the annual purchase of eighty thousand slaves, destined for colonies, is alone proprietor of two thirds of the commerce.

It is said that in all times there have been slaves, but in all times there have been robbers and wretches.—Bad examples can never make bad actions lawful. Cugoano establishes a comparison between ancient and modern slavery, and proves that the last, which prevails among christians, is worse than that among pagans, and still worse than that among the Hebrews, who did not steal men to enslave them, who did not sell them without their consent, and who put no fine on the head of fugitives. In Deuteronomy, it is formally said, "Thou shalt not deliver up to thy master a fugitive slave, who, in thy house, has sought an asylum." At the expiration of the seventh year, which was jubilee, a man had a right to freedom. In a word, slavery among the Hebrews was nothing more than a temporary vassalage.

From the old testament, the author passes to the new, and discusses with equal success, facts and principles, and the superiority is evident which his arguments derive from that celestial morality, that commands us to love our neighbour as ourselves, and to do to another that which we wish he would do to us. I could wish, says he, for the honour of christianity, that the odious art of stealing men had been known to Pagans.[18] He ought to say, for the honour of christians; for their crimes attach no more blame to religion, than the prevarication of judges to justice.—Then his arguments are not only applicable to the English clergy, but also to those of the Catholic church.

The clergy, by their vocation, are the messengers of justice—they ought to watch our society, expose its errors, and bring back the wicked to truth and virtue; if their conduct be otherwise, the public sins will fall upon their head. It is therefore evident, that the ecclesiastics do not know truth, or they dare not reveal it, and are therefore partners in national crimes.

He might have added, that adulation and baseness, are vices concerning which the clergy are never instructed, and of which they have almost always shewn the example. We know the conduct and the answer of St. Ambrosius to Theodorus of *Basil,* at Valens; others have occupied their places, but they have had no successors. Although the general opinion is, that Bossuet was not a prelate of the court, but a prelate at the court; yet his answer to the question of Louis the 14th, concerning comedy, perhaps shewed a little of the courtizan, and not enough of the bishop.

The good Cugoano, had every where seen temples erected to the God of the christians, and ministers charged with the task of repeating his precepts on them, and how could he believe that the children of the gospel could trample under foot the morals contained in the book which is the depositary of the divine oracles? He had too good an opinion of Europeans, and this error which does honour to his heart, is to them another disgrace.

Capitein

James Elizajohn Capitein, born in Africa, was bought at seven, or eight years of age, on the borders of the river St. André, by a negro trader, who made a present of him to one of his friends. The latter named him Capitein; he instructed, baptized him, and brought him to Holland, where he acquired the language of that Country. He devoted his time to painting, for which he had a great inclination. He commenced his studies at the Hague. Miss Boscam, a pious and learned lady, who, in this respect resembled Miss Schurman, was much occupied with the study of languages, she taught him the Latin, the elements of the Greek, Hebrew and Chaldaen tongues. From the Hague he went to the university of Leyden, and found every where zealous protectors. He devoted himself to theology under able professors, with the intention of returning home, to preach the Gospel to his Countrymen.[19] Having studied four years, he took his degrees, and in 1742, was sent as a Calvinist Minister to Elmina, in Guinea. In 1802, an English Journal, upon the authority of Motzere, minister of the Gospel at Harlem, spread a vague report, that Capitein, having returned to Guinea, had there abjured Christianity and embraced the worship of his country. This anecdote has been told in a less direct manner, in a letter addressed to me, by *de Vos,* a mennonite minister at Amsterdam, the author of some good works against negro slavery and duelling. He says that *Capitein,* who was so much praised before his departure, and whose engraved portrait was circulated throughout Holland, did not support his reputation; that on his return to Europe, some unpleasant news was spread concerning the immorality of his conduct: it is asserted, says he, that he was not far from abjuring Christianity.[20] If the first article be true, the second is probable; as, like so many others, he would become an unbeliever that he might with more ease act in opposition to the morality of the Gospel. But are his reproaches well founded? De Voss himself attenuates the force of the information, by the doubtful manner in which he expresses himself: and Blumenbach has written to me, and has since repeated, that having made enquiries on this head, he had not found any information against Capitein, whose portrait he had caused to be engraved in his work on the variety of the human figure.[21]

The first work of Capitein is an elegy in Latin verse, on the death of Manger, minister at the Hague, his preceptor and his friend—It is as follows.—

Hac autem in Batavorum gratissima sede
Non primum tantum elementa liaguæ Belgicœ
Addidici, sed arti etiam pictorica, in quam
Eram pro pensissimus, dedi operam Virum
Interea tempore labente, institutioni sua
Domestica catechesios mihi interesse permisit
Vir humanissimus, Joannes Phillipus Manger,
Cujus in obitum (cum tanti viri, tum
Solidor eruditionis, tum erga deum singularis
Pictatis, admirator semper extitissem) flebilibus
Fatis. Cum Ecclesior Hagienis protento anno

Esset ademptus, lugubrem hanc compersui
Elegiam!

Elegia

Invida mors totum vibrat sua tela per orbem:
Et gestit quemvis succubuisse sibi.
Illa, metùs expers, penetrat conclavia regum:
Imperiique manu ponere sceptra jubet.
Non sinit illa diù partos spectare triumphos:
Linquere sed cogit, clara tropœa duces.
Divitis et gazas, aliis ut dividat, omnes,
Mendicique casam vindicat illa sibi.
Falce senes, juvenes, nullo discrimine, dura,
Instar aristarum, demittit illa simul.
Hic fuit illa audax, nigro velamine tecta,
Limiua Mangeri sollicitare domŭs.
Hujus ut ante domum steterat funesta cypressus.
Luctisonos gemitus nobilis Haga dedit.
Hune lacrymis tinxit gravibus carissima conjux,
Dum sua tundebat pectora sæpe manu.
Non aliter Naomi, cum te viduata marito,
Profudit la crymas, Elimeleche, tua.
Sæpe sui manes civit gemebunda mariti,
Edidt et tales ore tremente sonos;
Cendit ut obscuro vultum velamine Phœbus,
Tractibus ut terræ lumina grata neget;
O decus immortale meum, mea sola voluptas!
Sic fugis ex ocalis in mea damna meis.
Non equidem invideo, consors, quod te ocyor aura
Transtulit ad lœtas æthereas que domos.
Sed quoties mando placidæ mea membra quieti,
Sive dies veniat, sum memor usque tui.
Te thalamus noster raptum mihi funere poscit.
Quis renovet nobis fœdera rupta dies?
En tua sacra deo sedes studiisque dicata,
Te propter, mæsti signa doloris habet.
Quod magis, effusas, veluti de flumine pleno,
Dant lacrymas nostri pignora cara tori.

Dentibus ut misere fido pastore lupinis
Conscisso teneræ disjiciuntur oves,
Aeraque horrendis, feriunt ɔalatibus altum,
Dum scissum adspiciunt voce cientque ducem:
Sic querulis nostras implent ululatibus ædes
Dum jacet in lecto corpus inane tuum.
Succinit huic vatum viduæ pia turba querenti,
Funera quæ celebrat conveniente modo
Grande sacerdotum decus, et mea gloria cessat,
Delicium domini, gentis amorque piæ!
Clauditur os blandum sacro de fonte rigatum;
Fonte meam possum quo relevare sitim!
Hei mihi? quam subito fugit facundia linguæ,
Cælesti dederat quæ mihi melle frui.
Nestoris eloquium veteres jactate pœtæ
Ipso Mangerius Nestore major erat, etc.

Capitein, at his admission to the university of Leyden, published a Latin dissertation on the calling of the Gentiles,[22] divided into three parts. He therein establishes, by the authority of the sacred writings, the certainty of the promise which embraces all nations, although the gospel cannot manifest itself but in a gradual manner, he proposes, that for the purpose of cooperating in this respect with the design of the Almighty, the languages of those nations should be cultivated to whom this blessing is yet unknown; and also that missionaries be sent among them, who, by the mild voice of persuasion, would gain their affections, and dispose them to receive the evangelical light.

The Spaniards, and still more the Portuguese, observe a milder and better conduct towards slaves. Amongst them the christian religion inspires a paternal character, which brings the slave nearer to his master. They have not established their superiority of colour, and they do not disdain to unite in marriage with negresses, and thus assist slaves in regaining their freedom.

In other colonies it has often happened, that planters have prevented their negroes from being instructed in a religion which proclaims the equality of men; all proceeding from a common stock—all participating the benefits of creation, and amongst whom, with the Father of men, their is no acceptation of persons. A number of writers have demonstrated this in the most evident manner. Of those in our times, it is sufficient to cite Robert Robinson,[23] Hayer, Roustan, Ryan, translated in French by Boulard. Turgot, in an excellent discourse, which Dupont de Nemours, communicated to me, and which he proposes to publish, entitled, *Political tyranny and slavery, are an outrage against Christianity.* The low adulation of a great number of bishops and priests, could not introduce other maxims than those in opposition to religion.

The Dutch planters, persuaded that the Christian religion is inconsistent with slavery, but stifling the voice of conscience, perhaps instigated Capitein to become the apologist of a bad cause. This negro believing, or feigning to believe, that by the support of slavery, we favour the propagation of the gospel, composed a politico-theological dissertation, to prove that slavery is not opposed to Christian freedom.[24] This scandalous assertion has been revived in America within a few years. A minister, named John Beck, in 1801, dared to preach and print two sermons to justify slavery.[25] Thanks to Humphrey, for having affixed the name of John Beck to the post of infamy.[26]

The author, Capitein, does not dissemble the difficulty of his undertaking, and more particularly in explaining the text of St. Paul; *you have been redeemed: be slaves to no person.*[27] He supposes, (I do not say he proves,) that this decision excludes only engagements made with idolatrous masters, to become gladiators, and fight in the arena with ferocious beasts,[28] as was the custom among the Romans. He cites, and without a comment, the famous edict of Constantine, which authorised the manumission of slaves, and the christian usage mentioned in the writings of the fathers, of giving freedom to slaves, particularly on Easterday.[29] From all quarters we hear the cry of history in favour of the freedom of slaves; the formalities of which are mentioned in Marcelsus; and because the law was only the license of the Pope, Capitein infers the lawfulness of slavery. This is evidently a forced conclusion.

He takes advantage of the testimony of Busbec, to prove that the destruction of slavery has not existed without great inconveniences, and that if the practice had continued, we would not see so many crimes committed, nor so many scaffolds erected for individuals who have nothing to lose;[30] but slavery inflicted as a lawful punishment, cannot make negro slavery lawful, and of this the authority of Busbec is nothing less than a proof.

This Latin dissertation of Capitein, rich in erudition, though poor in argument, was translated into Dutch, by Wilheur, with the portrait of the author as a frontispiece, in the dress of a minister,[31] and has gone through four editions. All that we can infer with reason from the sophisims of this negro, (to whom his countrymen will assuredly not bestow a vote of thanks) is, that a people under an unjust slavery, ought to be resigned to their unhappy lot, when they are unable to break asunder their chains.

Capitein also published a small volume in 4to. of Sermons in the Dutch Language, preached in different towns, and printed at Amsterdam, in 1742,[32] and Gallendot, who in the memoirs of the Academy of Flushing, has published an essay on the slave trade, discovers little judgment in praising the work of Capitein.[33]

Francis Williams

The information concerning this negro poet, has been taken partly from the *History of Jamaica,* by Long, who will not be suspected of partiality to negroes; for his prejudice against them shews itself even in the eulogium which was forced from him by truth.

Francis Williams, the son of negro parents, was born in Jamaica, toward the end of the 17th or the beginning of the 18th century. For he died at the age of 70, a short time before the publication of Long, which appeared in 1774.

Struck with the precocity of talents in the young negro, the duke of Montaigue, governor of the isle, proposed to try, whether by an improved education, he would be equal to a white man, placed in the same circumstances. Francis Williams being sent to England, commenced his studies in private schools, and afterwards entered the university of Cambridge, where, under able professors, he made considerable progress in mathematics. During his stay in Europe he published a Song, which commences thus:—

"Welcome, welcome, brother debtor."

This Ballad was so much in vogue in England, that certain individuals, irritated to see such merit in a black, attempted, but without success, to claim it as their own.

Francis Williams having returned to Jamaica, his protector, the duke of Montaigue, tried to obtain a place for him in the council of the government. This was refused. Williams then opened a school, in which he taught Latin and mathematics. He was preparing as his successor, a young negro, who unfortunately became deranged. Long cites this fact as a demonstrative proof that African heads are incapable of abstruse researches, such as problems in high geometry; although he supposes that the negro creoles have more capacity than the natives of Africa. Certainly if a particular fact would admit of a general induction, as the exercise of the intellectual faculties has proportionally deranged more heads among the learned and men of letters, than among other classes of society, it might be concluded that no one is capable of profound meditation.

But Long refutes himself; for, obliged to acknowledge in Francis Williams a talent for mathematics, he might with as much justice have drawn a conclusion directly contrary.

The historian pretends that Williams had no respect for his parents: that he was rude, and almost cruel to his children and his slaves. He wore a particular dress and a large wig to give a high idea of his knowledge.—He described himself to be a white man with a black skin, for he despised men of colour, and often said, shew me a negro, and I will shew you a thief. He was also of opinion that a negro and a white man, each perfect in his species, is superior to mulattoes formed of a heterogeneous mixture. This portrait of Williams may be true, but we must recollect that it was not executed by a friendly hand.

It appears that Williams had written many pieces in Latin verse. He loved this species of composition, and he was in the habit of presenting addresses of this kind to the new governor. That which he sent to Holdane is inserted in Long's history, who criticises it too severely. Williams having applied to his muse the epithet *Higernina,* Long indulges in low pleasantry concerning the introduction of this new personage into the family of the nine sisters, and he calls her madam *Æthiopissa.* He reproaches the author as a plagiarist, not in ideas, nor in phrases, but in the use of certain expressions, which as they are found in the best poets of antiquity, and also in dictionaries, it is blaming him for making Latin verses with Latin words. He reproaches him for comparing the members of the new government with the heroes of antiquity: this accusation is better founded. Unfortunately it applies to almost all poets. Have they not flattered one of the most criminal and contemptible men of Rome to such a degree, that the name of Mecenas is become classical among the English themselves, if we except Akenside, Pope, and some other poets, are they not, in this respect, all Wallers?

Nickolls seeing this Latin ode, and feeling indignant against the colonists for comparing blacks with apes, exclaimed—*I have never heard, that an ourang outang has composed an ode.*[34] "Among the defenders of slavery, we do not find, (says he,) one half of the literary merit of Phillis Wheatley and Francis Williams."

That the reader may be able to appreciate the talents of the last, we subjoin this Latin production, with a translation in French prose, and also one in English verse, which the historian Long thought it his duty to execute, notwithstanding his prejudices against the author.

> Integerrimo et fortissimo viro
> George Holdano, armigero,
> Insulæ Jamaicensis gubernatori;
> Cui omnes, morum, virtutumque dotes bellicarum,
> In cumulum accesserunt.[35]

Carmen

> Denique venturum fatis volventibus annum,[36]
> Cuncta per extensum læta videnda. diem,
> Excussis adsunt curis, sub imagine [37] clarâ
> Felices populi, terraque lege virens.

> [38]Te duce,[39] quæ fuerant malesuada mente peracta
> Irrita conspectu non reditura tuo.
> Ergo omnis populus, nec non plebecula cernet
> Hæsurum collo te[40] *relegasse* jugum,
> Et mala, quæ diris quondam cruciatibus, insons
> Insula passa fuit; condoluisset onus,
> Ni vixtrix tua Marte manus prius inclyta, nostris
> Sponte[41] ruinossis rebus adesse velit.
> Optimus es servus regi servire Britanno,
> Dum gaudet genio[42] scotica terra tuo:
> Optimus herôum populi[43] fulcire ruinam;
> Insula dum superest ipse[44] superstes eris.
> Victorem agnoscet te *Guadaloupa,* suorum
> Despiciet[45] merito diruta castra ducum.
> Aurea vexillis flebit jactantibus[46] *Iris,*
> Cumque suis populis, oppida victa gemet.

Crede, meum non est, vir Marti chare,[47] *Minerva*
Denegat *Æthiopi* bella sonare ducum.
Concilio, caneret te *Buchananus* et armis,
Carmine *Peleidæ,* scriberet ille parem.
Ille poeta, decus patriæ, tua facta referre
Dignior,[48] altisoni vixque *Marone* minor.
[49]Flammiferos agitante suos sub sole jugales[50]
Vivimus; eloquium deficit omne focis.
Hoc demum accipias multa fuligine fusum
Ore sonatura; non cute, corde valet.
Pollenti stabilita manu, Deus almus, oandem
Omnigenis animam, nil prohibente dedit.
Ipsa coloris egens virtus, prudentia; honesto
Nullus inest animo, nullus in arte color.
Cur timeas, quamvis, dubitesve, nigerrima celsam
Gæsaris occidui, scændere[51] *Musa* domum?[52]
[53]Vade salutatum, nec sit tibi causa pudoris,
[54]*Candida quod nigra corpora* pelle geris!
Intergitas morum[55] *maurum* magis ornat, et ardor
Ingenii et docto[56] *dulcis in ore decor:*
Hune, mage cor sapiens, patriæ virtutis amorque
[57]Eximit è sociis, conspicuumque facit,
[58]Insula me genuit, celebres aleure *Britanni*
Insula, te salvo non dolitura[59] patre!
Hoc precor[60] ô nullo videant te fine regentem
Florentes populos, terra, deique locus.

Franciscus Williams

The same translated.

To
That Most Upright and Valiant Man,
George Holdane, Esq.
Governor of the Island of Jamaica:
Upon Whom
*All Military and Moral Endowments Are
Accumulated.*

An Ode

At length revolving fates th' expected year
Advance, and joy the live long day shall cheer;
Beneath the fost'ring law's auspicious dawn
New harvests rise to glad the enliven'd lawn.[61]
With the bright prospect blest, the swains repair
In social bands, and give a loose to care.
Rash councils now, with each malignant plan,
Each faction, that in evil hour began,
At your approach are in confusion fled;
Nor while you rule, shall raise their dastard head.
Alike the master and the slave shall see
Their neck reliev'd, the yoke unbound by thee.
Till now, our guiltless isle, her wretched fate
Had wept, and groan'd beneath the oppressive weight
Of cruel woes, save thy victorious hand,
Long form'd in war, from Gallia's hostile land:
And wreaths of fresh renown, with generous zeal
Had freely turn'd, to prop our sinking weal.
Form'd as thou art, to serve Britannia's crown;
While Scotia claims thee for her darling son.
Oh! best of heroes, ablest to sustain
A falling people, and relax their chain.
Long as this isle shall grace the western deep
From age to age, thy fame shall never sleep.
Thee, her dread victor, Guadaloupe shall own,
Crush'd by thy arm, her slaughtered chiefs bemoan—
View their proud tents all levell'd in the dust,
And while she grieves, confess the cause was just.
The golden *iris* the sad scene will share,
And mourn her banners scatter'd in the air—
Lament her vanquish'd troops with many a sigh,
Nor less to see her towns in ruins lie.
Favorite of *Mars!* believe the attempt were vain,
It is not mine to try the arduous strain.
What! shall an Æthiop touch the martial string
Of battles, leaders, great achievements sing
Ah no! Minerva, with the indignant *nine*,

Restrain him, and forbid the bold design.
To a *Buchanan* does the theme belong—
A theme, that well deserves *Buchanan's* song.
'Tis he should swell the din of war's alarms,
Record thee great in council, as in arms:
Recite each conquest by thy valor won,
And equal thee to great *Peleides'* son.
That bard, his country's ornament and pride,
And who with *Mars* might e'en the bays divide:
Far worthier he, thy glories to rehearse,
And paint thy deeds in his immortal verse.
We live, alas! where the bright God of day,
Full from the zenith whirls his torrid ray:
Beneath the rage of his consuming fires,
All fancy melts, all eloquence expires.
Yet may you deign to accept this humble song,
Tho' wrapt in gloom, and from a falt'ring tongue;
Tho' dark the stream on which the tribute flows,
Not from the *skin,* but from the *heart* it rose.
To all of human kind, benignant heaven,
(Since nought forbids) one common soul has giv'n,
This rule was 'stablish'd by the eternal mind;
Nor virtue's self, nor prudence are confin'd,
To *colour,* none imbrues the honest heart;
To science none belongs, and none to art:
Oh! *muse* of blackest tint, why shrinks thy breast,
Why fears to approach the *Cæsar* of the *West*!
Dispel thy doubts, with confidence ascend
The regal dome, and hail him for thy friend:
Nor blush, altho' in garb funereal drest
Thy body's white, tho' clad in *sable vest.*
Manners unsullied, and the radiant glow
Of genius, burning with desire to know;
And learned speech, with modest accent worn
Shall best the sooty *African* adorn.
A heart with wisdom fraught, a patriot flame,
A love of virtue—these shall lift his name
Conspicuous, far beyond his kindred race,
Distinguished from them by the foremost place.

In this prolific isle I drew my breath
And Britain nurs'd:—illustrious thro' the earth.
This my lov'd isle, which never more shall grieve
Whilst you, our common friend, our father live.
Then this my prayer "May earth and heaven survey
A people ever blest beneath thy sway."

Francis Williams

Vassa

Olandad Equiano, better known by the name of Gustavus Vassa, was born in 1746, at *Essaka*. This is the name of a beautiful and charming valley, far distant from the coast and capital of Benin, of which it is considered as forming a part, although its government is almost independent, under the authority of some elders or chiefs, of which his father was one.

At the age of 12, Vassa was carried off with his sister, when children, by robbers, torn from their native soil, and from the arms of those to whom they owed their existence. The barbarians soon deprived him of the consolation of mingling his tears with those of his sister. Forever to be separated from her, he was thrown into a Guinea vessel, and, after a passage, the horrors of which he relates, he was sold at Barbadoes, and resold to a lieutenant of a vessel, who brought him directly to England; he accompanied him to Guernsey, to the siege of Louisbourg, in Canada, by Admiral Boscawen, in 1758, and to the siege of Belle-isle, in 1761.

Events having brought him back to the new world, by perfidy he was again put in irons. Vassa, sold at Montserrat, the sport of fortune, sometimes free, sometimes a slave, or domestic, made several voyages to most of the Antilles, and to different parts of the American continent. He returned several times to Europe, visited Spain, Portugal, Italy, Turkey, and Greenland. The love of freedom, which he had first felt in infancy, tormented his mind, and this torment was increased by the obstacles which prevented him from recovering it. He had vainly hoped that a firm zea for the interests of his master would be the sure means of obtaining this advantage; justice would there have found another reason for breaking his chains, to avarice it was a motive for rivetting them closer. With men devoured by an insatiable thirst for gold, he saw that he must have recourse to other means. Then commencing the most rigid economy, with three pence he began a small trade which gave him a tolerable profit, notwithstanding the injuries he sustained by the roguery of the whites; at last in 1781, having escaped the dangers of the sea, being several times shipwrecked, and having also avoided the cruelty of his masters, one of whom, at Savannah, proposed to assassinate him; after 30 years of a wandering and stormy life, Vassa, restored to liberty, established himself at London, where he married and published his memoirs,[62] which have been several times reprinted in both hemispheres, and of which there was a new edition in 1794. It is proven by the most respectable testimony that he was the Author. This precaution is necessary for a class of individuals who are always disposed to calumniate negroes to extenuate the crime of oppressing them.

The work is written with that *naivete,* I had almost said, that roughness of a man of nature. His manner is that of Daniel de Foe, in his Robinson Crusoe: it is that of Jameira Duval, who from the rank of a cow-keeper to hermits, became Librarian to Francis the first, and whose unprinted memoirs, so worthy of publication, are in the hands of Ameilhon.

We share the feelings of surprise which Vassa experienced at the shock of an earthquake, the appearance of snow, a picture, a watch and a quadrant, and the manner with which he interrogates his reason concerning the use of those instruments. To him the art of navigation had an inexpressible charm; for in this he saw the means of one day escaping from slavery. He made an agreement with the captain of a vessel to give him lessons, which were often interrupted, but the activity and intelligence of the scholar supplies all. Doctor Irving, with whom he had lived as servant, had taught him the method of rendering seawater fresh by distillation. Some time afterwards Vassa belonged to an expedition, the object of which was to find a passage to the North. In a moment of distress, he employed the process of the Doctor, and furnished a potable water to the crew.

Although carried from his country when young, his affection for his family, and a good memory preserved for him a rich store of recollections. We read with interest the description he has given of his country, where luxuriant nature has been prodigal of her bounties. Agriculture is the principal occupation of the inhabitants, who are very industrious, although they are passionately fond of Poetry, Music and Dancing.

Vassa recollects well that the Physicians of Benin drew blood by means of cupping glasses; that they excel in the art of healing wounds, and overcoming the effect of poisons. He presents a curious picture of the superstitions and habits of his country, which he contrasts with those of countries where he has travelled. Thus he finds among the Greeks, at Smyrna, the dances common at Benin: he discovers a resemblance between the customs of Jews, and those of his fellow countrymen, among whom circumcision is generally admitted. To touch a dead body is there considered as a legal impurity, and the women are accustomed to the same ablutions as the Hebrews.

The effect of adversity often is to give more energy to religious sentiments. Man abandoned by his fellow man, and unfortunate upon the earth, turns his looks towards heaven, to seek there consolation and a father. Such was Vassa; he did not sink under the load of evils which pressed upon him. Like Pluche, and other celebrated men, penetrated with the presence of the supreme Being, he continually directed his views beyond the bounds of life, towards a new country, *where all cries shall cease, where all tears shall be wiped away.*

A long time uncertain concerning his choice of a religion, he was shocked to see in all christian societies, a number of individuals whose actions are in direct opposition to their principles; who blaspheme the name of that God, of whom they profess themselves the adorers. For example, he feels indignant that the king of Naples and his court should go every Sunday to the opera. He sees some observe four, others six or seven precepts of the decalogue, and he cannot conceive how a man can be half virtuous. He knew not, that, as Nicols has said, we can know nothing of the doctrine by the conduct; nor of the conduct by the doctrine. Having long wandered in uncertainty, he was baptized in the English church, and became a Methodist, and he was on the point of being sent as missionary to Egypt. Taught by adversity, Vassa became very sensible to the misfortunes of others, and no one more than he, could with more propriety adopt the celebrated maxim of Terence. He deplores the fate of the Greeks, who are treated by the Turks almost in the same manner as the Negroes are by the colonists. He has sympathy even for the galley slaves, with whom the bounds of just punishment have been transgressed.

He had seen his African countrymen exposed to all the punishments which cupidity and rage have invented. He contrasts their cruelty with the morality of the gospel, which are in direct opposition. He proposes a plan of commerce between Europe and Africa, which at least would not wound justice. In 1789, he presents to the parliament of England a petition for the suppression of the slave trade. If Vassa still lived, the bill which was lately passed, would be consoling to his heart and his old age. That individual is to be pitied, who, after having read the memoirs of Vassa, does not feel for the author, sentiments of affection and esteem. His son, named *Sancho,* versed in Bibliography, is an assistant librarian to Sir Joseph Banks, and is also secretary to the committee for Vaccination. I shall terminate this notice with observing, that Vassa published a poem containing 112 verses, which he composed in consequence of his disquietude arising from a choice of a religion.

Sancho

The mother of Ignatius Sancho, thrown into a vessel on the coast of Guinea, employed in the slave trade, and destined for the Spanish possessions in America, was delivered of Sancho during the voyage. Arrived at Carthagena, he was baptized there by a bishop, named Ignatius. The change of climate soon conducted his mother to the tomb, and his father, delivered up to the horrors of slavery, in a moment of despair, terminated his existence with his own hand.

Ignatius was not two years of age when he was carried to England by his master, who made a present of him to three young ladies, sisters, residing at Greenwich. His character, which was supposed to resemble that of the knight of Don Quixot, induced them to give him this name.—The young Sancho was fortunate enough to attract the attention of the Duke of Montague, who resided at Black-Heath. This gentleman admired in him a frankness, which was neither degraded by servitude, nor corrupted by a false education. He often called him to him, lent him books, and advised his sisters to improve his genius, but from them Sancho had an opportunity of discovering, that ignorance is one of the means by which African slavery is promoted, and he discovers the opinion of planters, that to instruct, is to emancipate negroes. Often they threatened to send him back to slavery. The love of freedom which agitated his heart, was increased by study and meditation. He harboured a violent passion for a young female, which drew upon him another kind of reproach from the sisters. He then resolved to quit their house. But the Duke, his patron, was no more. Sancho, reduced to misery, employed five shillings (it was all he had) to purchase an old pistol, with which to terminate his days, as his father had done.—The Dutchess, who at first received him coldly, but who still esteemed him, employed him in the quality of butler. He remained in this situation till the death of his patroness. By his economy, and by a legacy left him by this lady, he found himself possessor of 70 pounds sterling, and thirty of an annuity.

With a fondness for study, he sometimes mingled that of the theatre, of women, and gambling. He renounced cards in consequence of a Jew having won all his clothes. He spent his last shilling at Drury-lane to see Garrick, of whom afterwards he became the friend. He then proposed to represent some character in *Othello* and *Oronoko,* but a bad articulation prevented him from succeeding in a situation which he considered as a resource against adversity.—He engaged in the service of the chaplain of the family of Montague, and his conduct becoming very regular, obtained him the hand of a very interesting female, born in the West Indies.

In 1773, by attacks of the gout and the smallness of his fortune, he would have again been plunged in misery, if the generosity of his protectors and his economy had not afforded him the means of commencing an honest trade. By his own and his wife's industry he reared a numerous family. The public esteem was the price of his domestic virtues. He died the 15th of December, 1780. After his death, a fine edition of his letters was published, in 2 volumes 8vo. which were well received by the public, and of which there was a second edition in 1783, with the life of the author, and his portrait, designed by Bartolozzi, and engraved by Gainsborough. Some articles are inserted, which had appeared in the public journals.

Jefferson reproaches him for yielding too much to his imagination, whose excentric march, says he, is like to those fugitive meteors which dart through the firmament. He nevertheless acknowledges, that he has an easy style, and happy expression, and that his writings breathe the sweetest effusions of sentiment.[63] Imlay declares that he has not had an opportunity of reading them, but observes, that the error of Jefferson in his opinions concerning negroes, renders suspicious all that he says of Sancho.[64]

Letters are a specie of literature which is seldom susceptible of analysis, whether it be owing to the variety of subjects it embraces, or to the liberty which the author takes in grouping many subjects in the same letter, of examining some deeply, whilst others are slightly passed over, and often flying from his subject to finish by digressions. We read the letters of madam de Sevignè, but no one has ever attempted to analyse them.—We certainly cannot compare the African author's to her, except in that kind of writing for which madam de Sevignè is so distinguished—but after her there are still honorable places. The epistolary style of Sancho resembles that of Sterne, of which it has the beauties and defects. With him Sancho had formed an acquaintance. The third volume of the letters of Sterne contain a very fine one addressed to Sancho, in which he tells him that the varieties of nature in the human species do not cut asunder the bands of consanguinity: and he expresses his indignation that certain men wish to class a portion of their equals in the rank of brutes, that they may with impunity treat them as such.[65]

Sometimes he is trivial—sometimes heated with his subject, he is poetical; but in general he has the grace and lightness of the fancy style. He is playfully witty, when between the tyrannic empire of fashion on the one hand, and health and happiness on the other; he places the man of the world irrisolute in his choice.

He is grave when he exposes the motives by which Providence has given to genius poverty as a companion: pompous when interrogating nature, she every where points out to him the works and hand of the Creator.

"According to the plan of the Deity, commerce (said he) ought to render common to all the globe the productions of each country; it ought to unite nations by the sentiment of reciprocal wants of fraternal amity, and thus facilitate a general diffusion of the benefits of the gospel: but those poor Africans, whom Heaven has favoured with a rich and luxuriant soil, are the most unhappy of the human species by the horrible traffic in slaves; and this is performed by christians."

We recollect the tragical end of Dr. Dodd, condemned to death for forgery, and the whole of whose former life had been a model of wisdom. We regret his punishment, when we read the letter in which Sancho unfolds the reasons which prevented him from obtaining pardon.

Some of his moral assertions might be disputed, if his writings generally did not present a repeated homage to virtue. He inspires this sentiment in painting the dutchess of K—, tormented by conscience—the great *chancellor of the soul.* "Act then always in such a manner as to gain the approbation of your heart—to be truly brave, one must be truly good.—We have reason as a rudder, religion for our anchor, truth for our polar star, conscience as a faithful monitor, and perfect happiness as a recompense."

In the same letter, endeavouring to drive away recollections, which might expose his virtue to a new shipwreck, he exclaims, "why bring to mind those combustible matters, whilst rapidly glancing over my past years, I approach the end of my career? Have I not the gout, six children and a wife? O heaven, where art thou? You see that it is much more easy to preach than to act, but we know how to separate good from evil; let us arm ourselves against vice and act like a general in his camp, who ascertains the force and position of the enemy and places advance guards to avoid surprize, let us act so even in the ordinary course of human life; and believe me, my friend, that a victory gained over passion, immorality and pride, is more deserving of a *te deum,* than that which is obtained in the field of ambition and of carnage."[66]

I request the reader not to confine himself to the extracts we have read; they can give but an imperfect idea of the author—the more respectful the authority of Jefferson is, the more important is it to combat his judgment, which seems too severe.

Phillis Wheatley

Phillis Wheatley was stolen from Africa at seven or eight years of age, carried to America, and sold in 1761, to John Wheatley, a rich merchant at Boston. Of amiable manners, exquisite sensibility, and premature talents, she was so cherished by the family, that they not only freed her from those painful labours reserved for slaves, but also from the cares of the household. Passionately fond of reading, and delighting in the perusal of the scriptures, she rapidly attained a knowledge of the Latin language. In 1772, at nineteen years of age, Phillis Wheatley, the negress slave, published a little volume in English, of religious and moral poetry, which contains thirty-nine pieces. This work has run through several editions in England and in the United States; and to take away all pretext from malevolence, in saying that she was not the author, the genuineness of the publication was established in the first page of the volume, by a declaration of her master, of the governor, and lieutenant governor of the state, and of fifteen other respectable persons in Boston, who knew her talents and the circumstances of her life.

In 1775, she received from her master, her freedom. Two years afterwards she married a man of colour, who, in the superiority of his understanding, to that of other negroes, was also a kind of phenomenon. We are no less surprized to see her husband a grocer, become a lawyer, under the name of Doctor Peter, and plead before tribunals the cause of the blacks. The reputation he enjoyed procured him a fortune.

The sentimental Phillis, who according to the trivial expression, was brought up as a spoiled child, knew nothing of domestic affairs, and her husband proposed that she should learn the household art. He began with reproaches, which were followed by a harshness, the continuance of which afflicted her so much, that in 1780 she died of a broken heart. Her husband, by whom she had a child, which died when very young, survived her only three years.[67]

Jefferson, who appears unwilling to acknowledge the talents of negroes, even those of Phillis Wheatley, pretends that the heroes of the *Dunciad* are divinities, when compared with this African muse.[68] If we were disposed to cavil, we might say, that to an assertion, it is sufficient to oppose a contrary assertion; we might appeal to the judgment of the public, which is manifested by the collection made of the poetry of Phillis Wheatley: but a more direct refutation may be made, by selecting some portions of her works, which will give us an idea of her talents. This has been done by Clarkson,[69] Imlay[70] and other authors.

It was doubtless her acquaintance with the works of Horace, that induced her to commence like him with an Ode to Macenas,[71] whose protection poets secured by flattery. Their baseness throws a veil over his Augustus, by the same means, buried in oblivion the horrors of the Triumvirate. Phillis in this piece reminds us that Terence was her compatriot. It is not without merit; but we hasten to subjects more worthy of her muse. Almost all her poetical productions have a religious or moral cast—all breathe a soft and sentimental melancholy. Twelve relate to the death of friends. We are particularly pleased with her odes on the works of Providence, on virtue, humanity, to Neptune to a young painter, of her own color. On seeing his works she vents her grief on the sorrows of her countrymen.

> Remember, Christians, negroes black as Cain
> May be refin'd and join the Angelic train.

The reader will permit us to present to him some of the productions of Phillis.

On the Death of J. C. an Infant.

No more the flow'ry scenes of pleasure rise,
Nor charming prospects greet the mental eyes,
No more with joy we view that lovely face
Smiling, disportive, flush'd with ev'ry grace.

The tear of sorrow flows from ev'ry eye,
Groans answer groans, and sighs to sighs reply;
What sudden pangs shot thro' each aching heart.
When, *Death,* thy messenger dispatch'd his dart!
Thy dread attendants, all destroying *Pow'r,*
Hurried the infant to his mortal hour.
Could'st thou unpitying close those radiant eyes?
Or fail'd his artless beauties to surprize?
Could not his innocence thy stroke controul,
Thy purpose shake and soften all thy soul?

The blooming babe, with shades of *Death* o'erspread,
No more shall smile, no more shall raise its head;
But like a branch that from the tree is torn,
Falls prostrate, wither'd, languid, and forlorn.
"Where flies my *James,*" 'tis thus I seem to hear
The parent ask, "Some angel tell me where
"He wings his passage thro' the yielding air?"
Methinks a cherub bending from the skies
Observes the question and serene replies,
"In heav'n's high palaces your babe appears:
"Prepare to meet him, and dismiss your tears."
Shall not th' intelligence your griefs restrain,
And turn the mournful to the chearful strain?
Cease your complaints, suspend each rising sigh,
Cease to accuse the Ruler of the sky.
Parents, no more indulge the falling tear:
Let *Faith* to heav'n's refulgent domes repair,
There see your infant like a seraph glow:
What charms celestial in his numbers flow.
Melodious, while the soul-enchanting strain
Dwells on his tongue, and fills th' etherial plain?

Enough—forever cease your murm'ring breath;
Not as a foe, but friend, converse with *Death,*
Since to the port of happiness unknown
He brought that treasure which you call your own.
The gift of heav'n intrusted to your hand
Chearful resign at the divine command;
Not at your bar must sov'reign *Wisdom* stand.

An Hymn to the Morning.

Attend my lays, ye ever honour'd nine,
Assist my labours, and my strains refine;
In smoothest numbers pour the notes along,
For bright *Aurora* now demands my song.

Aurora, hail, and all the thousand dyes,
Which deck thy progress through the vaulted skies:
The morn awakes, and wide extends her rays,
On ev'ry leaf the gentle zephyr plays;
Harmonious lays the feather'd race resume,
Dart the bright eye, and shake the painted plume.

Ye shady groves, your verdant gloom display
To shield your poet from the burning day:
Calliope, awake the sacred lyre,
While thy fair sisters fan the pleasing fire:
The bow'rs, the gales, the variegated skies
In all their pleasures in my bosom rise.

See in the east th' illustrious king of day!
His rising radiance drives the shades away—
But Oh! I feel his fervid beams too strong,
And scarce begun, concludes th' abortive song.

To the Right Honourable William, Earl of Dartmouth, His Majesty's Principal Secretary of State for North America, etc.

Hail, happy day, when, smiling like the morn,
Fair *Freedom* rose *New-England* to adorn:

Long lost to realms beneath the northern skies
She shines supreme, while hated *faction* dies:
Soon as appear'd the *Goddess* long desir'd,
Sick at the view, she languish'd and expir'd:
Thus from the splendors of the morning light
The owl in sadness seeks the caves of night.
No more, *America,* in mournful strain
Of wrongs, and grievance unredress'd complain,
No longer shalt thou dread the iron chain,
Which wanton *Tyranny* with lawless hand
Had made, and with it meant t' enslave the land.

Should you, my lord, while you peruse my song,
Wonder from whence my love of *Freedom* sprung,
Whence flow the wishes for the common good,
By feeling hearts along best understood:
I, young in life; by seeming cruel fate
Was snatch'd from *Afric's* fancy'd happy seat:
What pangs excruciating must molest,
What sorrows labour in my parents' breast?
Steel'd was that soul, and by no misery mov'd,
That from a father seized his babe belov'd:
Such, such my case: And can I then but pray
Others may never feel tyrannic sway? etc. etc.

Notes

1. Joachim de Sandrat, Academia nobilissimœ artis pictoriœ, in fol. Norimbergæ, 1683. ch. 15, p. 34.

2. In 3 vols. fol. Nuremberg, 1675, 2d. part, the copy of which in the National Library, is on the outside, marked as the first.

3. Pliny, B. 35, ch. 17, et memoires de L'Academie des Inscriptions, § 35, p. 345.

4. Excussis tam veterum quam novorum placitis, optima quæque selegit selecta, enucleate ac dilucide interpretatus est.

5. Dissertatio inauguralis philosophica de humanæ mentis ΑΠΑΘΕΙΑ sue sensionis ac facultates sentiend in mente humana absentia et carum in corpore nostro organico ac vivo præsentia, quam præside, &c. publice defendit, autor, G. Amo, Guinea-afer. Philosophiœ, etc. L.C. magister, etc. 1734, 4to. Wittenbergœ. At the end are subjoined several pieces: The letters of Congratulation of the Rector, &c.

6. Disputatio philosophica continens ideam distinctam earum quæ competunt vel menti vel corpori nostro vivo et organico, quam consentiente amplissimorum philosophorum ordine, præside M. Ant. Guil. Amo, Guinea, afer, &c. defendit Joa. Theod. Mainer, Philos. et J. V. Cultor, 4to. 1734, Wittenbergæ.

7. Voyage autour du monde traduit de L'Itelien de Gemelli Carreri, in 12mo. Paris, 1719, vol. V, p.64, and following, p. 135, and following; also, L'Encyclopedie Methodique, art. Philippines.

8. Ibid. p. 142, 143.

9. Ueber die Tagalische sprache von Franz Carl Alters, &c. 8vo.Vienna, 1803.

10. P. 184.

11. Buchan.—Domestic Medicine, Paris, 1783, vol. III, p. 518.

12. Medecine du voyageur, par Duplaint, 3 vol. 8vo. Paris, vol. III, p. 272.

13. Narrative of a five years expedition against the revolted negroes of Surinam, &c. by capt. J. G. Stedman, 2 vols. 4to. London, 1796, vol. II, c. xxvi. French translation of this work, vol. III, p. 61, and following. In the question addressed to Fuller, the word *seconds* is forgotten, which renders it absurd.

14. American Museum, vol. V, p. 2.

15. Brissot. Ses voyages, vol. II, p. 2.

16. Clarkson, p. 125.

17. Ibid. p, 134, and following.

18. The English is perhaps the only language, which, to designate the acts of stealing children, has the word *kidnap*—the verb and its derivations.

19. Journal, called the Merchant, No. 31. August, 14, 1802.

20. Letter of Mr. de Vos to Mr. Gregoire, 27, 1801.

21. Letter of Mr. Blumenbach to Mr. Gregoire.

22. De vocatione Ethnicorum.

23. Slavery inconsistent with the spirit of christianity, a sermon preached at Cambridge, by Robert Rabinson, 8vo. 1788. He affirms, page 14, that the Africans were the first to baptize their children in order to avoid slavery.

24. Dissertatio politico-theologica de servitute libertati christianæ non contraria, quam sub præside J. Van den Honert, publicæ disquisitioni subjicit, J.T.J. Capitein, afer, 4to. Lugduní Batavorum, 1742.

25. The doctrine of perpetual bondage reconciliable with the infinite justice of God; a truth plainly asserted in the Jewish and christian scripture, by John Beck.

26. A valedictory discourse delivered before the Cincinnati of Connecticut, in Hartford, July 4th, 1804, at the dissolution of the society, by D. Humphrey, 8vo. Boston, 1804.

27. Cor. vii. 23. Pretio empti estis, nolite fieri servi hominum.

28. P. 27.

29. S. Gregory, de Hysse.

30. Epistola turcica, Lugduni Batavorum, 1633, p. 160, 161.

31. Staatkundig-godgeleerd onderzoeksschrift over de slaverny, als niet strydig tegen de christelike vriheid, &c. uit het latyn vertaalt door heer de Wilhelm, 4to. Leiden 1742.

32. Vit gewrogte predicatien zynde de trowherrige vermaaninge van den apostel der heydenen Paulus, aan zynen zoon Timotheus vit. II. Timotheus, II, v. 8 te Muiderberger, den 20 mai 1742, alsmede de voornaamste goederen van de op-

perste wysheit spit sprenken VIII, v. 18, in twee predicatien in s'Gravenhage, den 27 mai 1742. en t'ouderkerk aan den Amstel, den 6 juny 1742, gedaan door J.E.J. Capitein, africaansche Moor, beroepen predikant op d'Elmina, aan het kasteel S. George, 4to. te Amsterdam.

33. Noodige onderrichtingen voor de slaafhandeiaaren, t. I. Verhandelingen vitgegeven door het zeeuwsch genootschap, etc. te Middleburg, 1769, p. 425.

34. Letter to the treasurer of the society instituted for the purpose of effecting the abolition of the slave trade, from the Rev. Robert Bouche Nickolls, Dean of Middleham, 8vo. London, 1738, p. 46.

35. The history of Jamaica, or general survey of the ancient and modern state of that Island, &c. in three Volumes, illustrated with copperplates, London, 1774, p. 478, 79, and 80.

36. *Aspice venturo lœtentui ut omnia sœclo, Virg. E. 4. 52.*

37. *Clara* seems to be rather an improper epithet joined to *imago.*

38. *Te duce,* si qua manent sulenris vestigia nostro *Irrita,* perpetua solvent formidine terras, Virg. E. 4. 13.

39. Alluding perhaps to the contest, about removing the seat of government and public offices from *Spanish Town to Kingston,* during the administration of the governor.

40. Pro rĕvĕlasse.

41. Quem vocet divum populus *ruentis* imperi rebus, Hor. B 1. ode 2.

42. Mr. Holdane was a native of North Britain.

43. In Ptolemea potes magni *fulcire* ruinam. Lucan. B. 8. § 28.

44. This was a promise of somewhat more than antediluvian longevity; but the poet proved a false prophet, for M. Holdane did not survive the delivery of this address many months.

45. Egerit *justo domitor* triumpho, Hor. B. 1. ode 12.

46. Phabus volentem prœlia me loqui victas et verber, increpuit lyra ne, Hor.

47. Invicta Minerva, Hor. de art. poet.

48. Maronis altisoni, cannina Juv. Set. 11. ver. 178.

49. *Flamini feras* rotas toto calo agitat.

50. I apprehend M. Williams mistook this for jŭbar, Sun beams.

51. This is a *petitio principii,* or begging the question, unless with Mr. Pope,—

All are but parts of one stupendous whole,
Whose body nature is, and God the soul:
But,
Far as Creation's ample range extends
The *scale* of *sensual mental* powers ascends.

52. M. Williams has added a *black muse* to the Pierian choir; and, as he has not thought proper to bestow a name upon her, we may venture to announce her by the title of Ethiopissa.

53. *Vade salutatum* subito perorata parentem litterra. *ovid.*

54. See his apothegms before mentioned.

55. *Maurus,* is not in classic strictness, proper Latin for a negro.

56. *Mollis* in ore *decor*—incert.

57.
Me doctorum edere prœmia frontium.

. . . .

. . . .
secemunt populo. Hor. 1 lib. ode 1.

58. Mantua me genuit, calabri rapuere. Virg.

59. Hic ames dici *pater* atque principi. Hor.

60. Serus in calum rededs, *duique Lœtus intersis popula, Hor.*

61. Lawn is here used in the sense given it by Johnson, viz. an open space between woods; which has a particular propriety applied to the corn fields in Jamaica.

62. The interesting Narrative of the life of Olando Equiano or Gustavus Vassa, the African, written by himself, 9th edit. 8vo. London, 1791, with the portrait of the Author.

63. Letters of the late Ignatius Sancho, an African, to which are prefixed memoirs of his life, 2 vol. 8vo. London, 1782.

64. Imlay, p. 215.

65. Letters of the Rev. Lawrence Sterne, to his intimate friend 8 vol. 8vo. London, 1775.

66. *Passim.* I vol. letter 7.

67. Letter from Mr. Giraud, French consul, at Boston, dated 8th October, 1805.

68. Notes on Virginia.

69. Clarkson, p. 121.

70. Imlay's Topographical Description, letter 9, p. 200 and following.

71. Poems on various subjects, religious and moral, by Phillis Wheatley, negro servant, 8vo. London, 1773.

Chapter VIII

Conclusion

Of all countries where science is cultivated, I doubt whether there be one so much a stranger to foreign literature as France. We need not therefore be surprized that no mention is made of negro authors, in our historical dictionaries, which are little else than financiering speculations. They contain a pompous list of ephemeral romances, and theatrical pieces long forgotten. A place is given to Cartouche, and Kaskes, the founder of *Sunday Schools,* is forgotten. No notice is taken of Hawes, the establisher of the Humane Society, for the recovery of individuals struck with apparent death: nor of Hartlib, Maitland, Long, Thomas Coram, Hanway, Fletcher of Salton, Enius Walter, Wagenaar, Buckelts, Meenwis Parker, Valentyn, Eguyara, Francis Solis, Mineo, Chiarizi, Tubero, Jerusalem and Finnus Johannacus, we do not find even the name of Suhm, the Puffendorf of the last century, nor that of many national writers who merit distinction, such as Persini, Blarn, Jehan de Brie, John de Lois, and the good Quaker Benizet, born at St. Quintin, the friend of all men, the defender of the oppressed, who, during his whole life, combatted slavery by reason, religion and example. He established, at Philadelphia, a school for young negroes, who were taught by himself. During those intervals of leisure which the functions of his employment allowed, he sought for the unfortunate to give them comfort. At his funeral, which was honoured with the solemn attendance of an immense number of people, an American colonel, who had served as engineer in the war of freedom, exclaimed, "I

111

would rather be Benizet in his coffin, than George Washington with all his celebrity." An exaggeration which does honour to his heart. In speaking of Benizet, Yvan Raiz, a Russian traveller, said, "the Academies of Europe resound with praises decreed to illustrious men, and the name of Benizet is not found on the list. For whom then do they reserve their crowns? This Frenchman, who so powerfully excited the attention of strangers, is not even known in France." His name is not mentioned by our compilers of dictionaries; but Benjamin Rush, and a number of English and Americans, have at least repaired this omission.

Men, who have consulted only their common sense, and who have not attended to discussions relative to colonies, will perhaps scarcely believe that many have classed negroes in the rank of brutes, and have questioned their moral and intellectual capacity. This doctrine, however, as absurd as it is abominable, is insinuated in different writings. It cannot be disputed that negroes, in general, to ignorance join absurd prejudices, gross vices, and especially those which belong to slaves of all species and all colors:—Frenchmen, Englishmen and Hollanders, what would you have been, if placed in the same circumstances? I maintain, that among errors the most stupid, and crimes the most hideous, there is not one for which you ought to reproach them.

In Europe, during ages, whites, under various forms, have made slaves of whites. Can we otherwise characterize the impressment of men in England, the conduct of *lady sellers* in Holland, and that of German Princes, who vend their regiments for the service of the colonies? But, if ever negroes, bursting their chains, should come, (which Heaven forbid) on the European coast, to drag whites of both sexes from their families; to chain them and conduct them to Africa, and mark them with a hot iron: if whites stolen, sold, purchased by crimes, and placed under the guidance of merciless inspectors, were immediately compelled, by the stroke of the whip, to work in a climate injurious to their health, where at the close of each day, they would have no other consolation than that of advancing another step to the tomb—no other perspective than to suffer and to die in all the anguish of despair—if devoted to misery and ignominy, they were excluded from all the privileges of society, and declared legally incapable of judicial action, their testimony would not have been admitted even against the black class:—if, like the slaves of Batavia, these white slaves in their turn, were not permitted to wear shoes and stockings—if driven from the side walks, they were compelled to mingle with the animals in the middle of the street—if a subscription were made to have them *lashed* in a mass, and their backs, to prevent gangrene, covered with pepper and with salt—if the forfeit for killing them were but a trifling sum, as at Barbadoes and Surinam—if a reward were offered for apprehending those who escape from slavery—if those who escape were hunted by a pack of hounds, trained to carnage—if, blaspheming the Divinity, the blacks pretended, that by their origin they had permission of heaven to preach passive obedience and resignation to the whites—if greedy hireling writers published, that for this reason, just reprisals may be exercised against the *rebellious* whites, and that white slaves are happy, more happy than the peasants in the bosom of Africa:—in a word, if all the arts of cunning and calumny, all the strength and fury of avarice, all the inventions of ferocity were directed against you, by a coalition of dogs, merchants, priests, kings, soldiers and colonists, what cry of horror would resound through these countries? To express it, new epithets would be sought; a crowd of writers, and particularly of poets, would exhaust their eloquent lamentations, provided that having nothing to fear, there was something to gain. Europeans, reverse this hypothesis, and see what you are!

During the three last centuries, tygers and panthers are less terrible to Africa, than you. For three centuries, Europe, which calls herself christian and civilized, tortures without pity, and without remorse, the people of Africa and America, whom she calls savage and barbarian. To procure indigo, sugar and coffee, she has introduced amongst them drunkenness, desolation, and a forgetfulness of all the sentiments of nature. Africa is not even allowed to breathe when the powers of Europe are combined to tear her to pieces. Yes, I repeat it, there is not a vice, not a species of wickedness, of which Europe is not guilty towards negroes, of which she has not shewn them the example. Avenging God! suspend thy thunder, exhaust thy compassion, in giving her time and courage to repair, if possible, these horrors and atrocities.

I have taken upon myself the task of proving, that the negroes are capable of virtues and talents; this I have established by reasoning, and still more by facts: these facts do not announce sublime discoveries; these works are not chef d'oeuvres, but they furnish irrefutable arguments against the enemies of negroes. I shall not say with Helvetius, that all individuals at their birth, have the same dispositions, and that man is the product of his own education: though this assertion, false in a general sense, is true in many respects. A union of fortunate circumstances unfolded the genius of Copernicus, Galileo, Leibnitz and Newton: perhaps others might have surpassed them, if unfortunate circumstances had not prevented the developement of their mind. Each country has its Baotia, but we may say, in general, that virtue and vice, wisdom and foolishness, genius and stupidity, belong to all countries, nations, heads and complexions.

To form a comparison of the people of different countries, we must place them in the same situation and circumstances; and what likeness can be found between whites, enlightened by the truths of christianity, (which leads to almost all others) enriched by the discoveries and information of all ages, and stimulated by every species of encouragement, and blacks, deprived of all those advantages, and devoted to oppression and misery? If some of them had not given a proof of their talents, there would be no reason for surprize; what astonishes us is, that so many of them have displayed genius. What would they then be, if restored to the dignity of free men, they occupied the rank which nature has assigned and tyranny refused?

Revolutions, in the political world, on account of the disasters they occasion, may be compared to the great convulsions of nature. The planters have been guilty of another imposture, in asserting that the friends of the blacks wished for a sudden and general freedom: It is not so, they were in favour of progressive measures, which, without commotion, would accomplish the desired object. Such was the opinion of the author of this work, when in a publication addressed to negroes and free mulattoes, which brought upon him so much abuse, he announced (and he still announces it) that one day, on the banks of the Antilles, the sun will shine on free men only, and its beams no longer set on irons and slaves. But the French planters have rejected with fury all the decrees by which the constituent assembly proposed to introduce gradually those salutary reforms: their pride, says Genty, has lost them the *new world,* which will never flourish but under the auspices of personal liberty. The horrible traffic which man there makes of his own species, will never lead to a durable prosperity.

Happily the colonies, and the American continent, the last asylum of liberty, are advancing to a state of things, which will be common to the Antilles, and whose course all the combined powers will be unable to arrest. Negroes, reinstated in their rights, by the irresistible force of events, will owe no gratitude towards colonists, whose affections might have been won by means equally easy and useful.

Manual labour, voluntarily undertaken, the utility of which is acknowledged in Brazil and the Bahamas, and the successful introduction of the plough in Jamaica[1] are sufficient to shew the order of overthrowing, or modifying the colonial system. This revolution will have an accelerated motion when industry and freedom, better acquainted with their mutual relations, shall call in the aid of the steam-engine and other mechanical inventions, which abridge labour and facilitate manipulations; when an energetic and powerful nation, to whom every thing announces a high destiny, stretching her arms across the Atlantic and Pacific Oceans, shall dart her vessels from the one to the other by a shorter rout, whether by cutting the isthmus of Panama, or by forming a canal of communication, as has been proposed, by the river St. John, and the lake of Nigaragua, and thus change the face of the commercial world, and of empires; who knows whether America will not avenge herself for the outrages she has suffered, and whether old Europe, reduced to the rank of a subaltern power, will not become a colony of the new world?

There is nothing useful but what is just: there is no law of nature which makes one individual dependent on another: and all these laws, which reason disavows, have no force. Every person brings with him into the world his title to freedom.[2] Social conventions have circumscribed its use, but its limits ought to be the same for all the members of a community, whatever be their origin, colour or religion. If, says *Price,* you have a right to make another man a slave, he has a right to make you a slave: and if we have no right, says *Ramsay,* to sell him, no one has a right to purchase him.[3]

May European nations at last expiate their crimes towards Africans. May Africans, raising their humiliated fronts, give spring to all their faculties, and rival the whites in talents and virtues only; avenging themselves by benefits and effusions of fraternal kindness, at last enjoy liberty and happiness. Although these advantages be but the dream of an individual, it is at least consoling to carry to the tomb the conviction, that we have done every thing in our power to procure them for others.

Notes

1. Dallas, vol. 1, pg. 4. Barré St. Venant also proposes to introduce the plough into the colonies.
2. Le Gente.
3. Essay on the treatment and conversion of slaves.

FINIS.

Index

This index lists the proper names of individuals mentioned by Grégoire in addition to key concepts and subjects. There are two editorial devices. First, in a number of places, Grégoire misspells proper names. Correct spellings are indicated in parenthesis after Grégoire's usage. Second, Grégoire often refers to individuals only by their last names. Wherever possible, I have silently added full names.

Graham Russell Hodges is Professor of Early American History at Colgate University. His many books and articles include *Slavery and Freedom in the Rural North: African Americans in Monmouth County, New Jersey, 1665–1870* (1996) and *The Black Loyalist Directory: African Americans in Exile in the Age of Revolution* (1995).